Colored Men Don't Ride Horses

Colored Men Don't Ride Horses

My Life from Jim Crow to North Idaho

an autobiography

SCOT
WRIT
PUBLISHING

Albert Wilkerson

with Amy Wilkerson

For permission requests, write to:
Scot Writ Publishing
PO Box 134
Gig Harbor, WA 98335-9998

scotwrit@gmail.com
facebook.com/AmyWilkersonAuthor

Library of Congress: 2020918246
ISBN: 978-1-7358232-0-1

My husband Albert's autobiography was completed only a few months before his death. After a time for grieving, I began reviewing the manuscript and found that much work remained to be done: editing, research, contacting folks, etc. I would like to thank those who contributed to his book in any way large or small but in particular, Rachel, Betsy and my daughter Sheila.

In Albert's name, I would like to thank all those who cared for him in life and in his passing and dedicate his book to family and friends.

—Amy

– 1 –

Early Days

It's 1944 in Birmingham, Alabama, the most segregated city in the country and Blacks typically went to the movies at the Carver Theater on Fourth Ave. However, sometimes, my father took my brother Leon and me to see a western in one of the theaters in the white section of town, where the only seats for us were in the balcony.

One evening, we set off by trolley to see a Wild Bill Elliot western, one of my favorites. We all enjoyed the film, but it was after 10 o'clock when we finally came out of the theater, too late to catch a trolley. Sometimes when the trolleys had stopped running, we walked home to our section of town on the railway tracks—up over a railway trestle—one that had no barrier and a long drop to the street below. Our father would hoist Leon on his shoulders, grip my hand in his, and tell me, "Don't look down."

But on that night, my father made a decision that was to dramatically change our lives. Since it was so late, he decided that we would take the shortest route home—through a white neighborhood.

Our dad began walking briskly with us, cutting through the dark streets, holding tightly to our hands—Leon on the left, me on the right. The white, residential neighborhood had big houses, with oak and magnolia trees. I was glad that we were not walking home over the scary train tracks, but the huge houses and oaks were almost as intimidating. Suddenly I was jolted out of imagining monsters in the shadows when I saw the outline of a man standing under a tree.

Early photos of Albert and his brother Leon.

My father gripped my hand a little tighter, and my body stiffened with fear as we started to walk past the man.

Then it came.

"BOY! What are you doing in this neighborhood?"

"Keep looking straight ahead," our dad warned us under his breath.

As the man came out from the shadow of the tree, I could see his police uniform in the street light. We walked on, but my heart beat faster as I heard steps coming up swiftly from behind. My father gripped my hand even more tightly.

"BOY. Did you hear me talking to you?"

The voice was close now. My father stopped.

"Are you talking to my boys?" he asked, speaking slowly, distinctly.

The white policeman grabbed my dad's left shoulder, and as my father pulled away, he dropped our hands and pushed us backward while the officer lifted his billy club to strike.

POW!

The sound of the slap was loud. My father had swung around and slapped the policeman on the left of his face so hard that the imprint was livid even in the street lamp. The policeman fell to one knee.

Out came my father's pocketknife in a flash, and he pressed the blade instantly against the throat of the policeman.

"My boys and I," said my father deliberately, controlling his anger, "were on our way home from a picture show, and we weren't bothering anyone. If you bother us anymore, I will cut your throat."

He paused.

"I'm taking my knife away now, and we're going home." He straightened up and took our hands. "Come on boys."

The policeman was still on the ground; his billy club still looped around his wrist, his Smith and Wesson in its holster and a look of shock and disbelief frozen on his face.

As we walked away, my stomach was tight and my shoulders rigid… I knew what was coming. But it never came. No shot rang out. There was just the echo of our footsteps on the sidewalk. There was no tragedy in our family that night in Birmingham, but it was the end of a period in my life which was one of the happiest I would ever know. Within a week, Leon, my dad, our stepmother and I left Birmingham in the dark and joined the Great Migration of Black families and headed north to safety.

From that evening on, it seems as though I was always looking over my shoulder, on guard and vigilant.

————◆————

Birmingham, Alabama had been my home for the first six years of my life. In a small duplex in the projects, in an all-Black neighborhood, I lived with Leon, my stepmother and my father, Albert Sr. He was the kind of father that anyone would love to have; athletic and strong, over six feet in height, with long arms and legs. He played with us, took us fishing and brought us downtown for a pair of shoes or to the cinema. He was a man of strong values who taught us well.

My stepmother, Ella Bea, was a nurse and worked nights. I have few early memories of her, unlike the vivid memories of my father, and I had no memory of my biological mother, Grace, who had left us with our father at a young age.

A typical Sunday morning when I was five and Leon three, would find us sitting at the wooden kitchen table with hands washed, waiting for the breakfast that our father cooked—the smell in the air of warm biscuits served with smothered veal and rice. We said grace before eating and had to remember our manners with elbows off the table and with a "please" or "no thank you" expected. Our dad drank black coffee with lots of sugar, and I anticipated the joy of sharing the last of my father's second cup of coffee, which was usually left on the table.

In the duplex next door, lived a woman who was also a nurse; a kind woman who liked Leon and me and who hired me to clear up her kitchen while she slept prior to the beginning of her late shift. I diligently swept the kitchen floor, wiped off the counters and washed her dishes. At only five years of age I couldn't reach the sink, so I stood on a blue-topped wooden stool industriously soaping and rinsing. One day disaster struck! The big, white serving bowl was too big and slick for my hands. As I struggled to keep my balance, the bowl slipped and crashed, breaking into a dozen pieces.

I was terrified. What would she do? What would my father think?

When my employer, the nurse, woke up, I spilled the beans and my pay was docked 25 cents per day.

One of my fondest memories is fishing with my father and Leon on the river. These fishing trips were exciting. We took along bologna, soda crackers, cheddar cheese (which I didn't like), and Pepsi Colas, in a brown paper sack for our lunch and then, from the bank of the river, my father cast the line from his cane pole into the water, and Leon and I played in the shadow of the trees. Nearby, the bottles of Pepsi Cola lay cooling in the water, fastened around their necks with twine to hold them against the swift current.

On one occasion, my dad caught an extraordinary fish in a most unusual way.

The fish that he went after was a giant catfish known to hide out in an underwater cave by the river bank. He dove in to the water with a rope as Leon and I watched, excited and anxious, asking, "How can he see under water? How can Daddy hold his breath so long?"

Below water, my father found and then cornered the giant catfish, wrestled the rope through its mouth and gills, and fought it to the surface and then on to the riverbank. I remember clearly the glistening, silver catfish with its barbells looking like long spiked whiskers. When our father held the fish up beside me, it was as tall as I was.

When we gutted the fish for dinner, we discovered over 50 hooks in its belly. In my eyes, my father was a legend.

One day my dad took us out to Centerville to meet his mother's side of the family: Aunt Minnie, Grandpa Oliver and his sister Bessie who were mixed race with white and Native American. To me, Grandpa Oliver looked like "an old white man"—tall, with pale skin, fierce gray-blue eyes, gray hair combed straight back and buttoned into a white shirt with one strap dangling from his bib overalls.

"Mr. Charlie" was a term that Blacks used referring to white men and, lo and behold, white-skinned Grandpa Oliver had a brother called Charlie. Years later I would see the humor in this.

My first impression of Grandpa Oliver was not as troublesome as my second visit.

After giving Grandpa a formal greeting, I went outside with Leon to play, and there in front of us in the front yard was a big black Packard with "a let-down top" tempting us to explore. I stepped on to the running board, opened the car door, got in and sat in the front seat. I started playing with the switches and then fiddled with the big lever that came up from the floorboard.

It released the brake.

The car was sitting on the crest of a hill and it started to roll—down the hill, faster and faster with me hanging on to the steering wheel. I was so panicked that it felt like my heart was in my mouth. The car picked up speed until it ran in to an oak tree that grew in the middle of the split in the driveway. On impact, the spring bumper caused the car to jolt backwards, and I was thrown forward over the steering wheel and into the hinged windshield which folded, banging down onto the hood of the car.

5

Grandpa Oliver was running after the car with a pace faster than I thought was possible for him. Out of breath, he grabbed me by one arm, whipping me off the car with an aggression that scared me half to death. I could smell the adrenaline on him as he hauled me back up the hill into the house, where he severely beat my bottom with a razor strap until I howled.

I already thought my grandfather was "white and scary" but I really did not like him from this point on, and throughout my life I have been leery of old, gray-headed white men.

During one visit, early one Sunday morning, we went to our cousin's house for breakfast. It was a two mile walk through the woods. Breakfast was corn bread in a bowl with fresh cow's milk poured over—as we ate the strange breakfast, Leon and I thought wistfully of our favorite Sunday breakfast that dad cooked for us at home.

I forgot all about this disappointing breakfast when our cousins took me outside to ride a horse for the very first time. Blackie was enormous. In the chilly morning air, vapor streamed from his nostrils.

"Can I ride Blackie?" I asked my cousin Archie. I was lifted onto Blackie's wide back as Archie led him around with a rope. I could feel the muscles of the horse under me; it felt strong, assuring and steady. I felt so confident that I had the urge to stand up, slowly and carefully, with my arms out. And there it was. I was in love with horses from that moment on.

When Leon and I visited our grandfather in the summer, we went with our cousin Richard—who was ten—to the mill, taking corn that had been scraped from the cob for grinding. Two bags of corn were tied with rope and slung over the back of a cow. At the mill, we stood in line until it was our turn for the big mill stone, then our ground corn was poured back into the sacks and lifted onto the back of the cow for the trek home.

One summer, Leon and I spent a few days with our Aunt Bessie. It was warm and we both wore short pants.

Aunt Bessie was a pretty lady who—like Grandpa Oliver—looked white, and she lived in a lovely cottage with pine trees all around. Every day she made a pot of tea and served Leon and me tea and teacakes. She was fun too. She showed us how to take a sheet of roof tin, form a wire handle and ride down the hill by her cottage on thick pine needles.

Bessie's sister Bonnie was even whiter. Aunt Bessie had brown hair and olive skin, but Bonnie had white skin and strawberry blonde hair. Years later Bonnie confessed to me that during the Depression she had passed for white; meaning that she had allowed white folk to assume she was white, to get by in grim times. This bothered me, because it seemed like she was ashamed of belonging to our family.

———•———

The nation was at war in the 1940's but my father had been declared 4F, and I don't remember any discussion of war at home.

Despite being unable to read and write, my father had a respectable job; he was a mortician, funeral director, and an ambulance driver for Poole's Funeral Chapels, one of the biggest Black funeral homes in Birmingham at the time. Poole's had a fleet of black Cadillac hearses and three ambulances. My brother and I often went with our father to work, and I didn't mind going there. I was OK with seeing dead people lying in their coffins after my father had embalmed them, but the occasional sight of corpses before they were embalmed in the morgue did bother me—although it didn't seem to bother Leon. Mr. Poole, the owner, liked us, called us, "Nice boys," and often produced a treat for us.

Albert Wilkerson, Sr.

Funeral homes, barbershops, and dry cleaners like "Famous" were Black-owned community businesses, but the owners of the grocery stores were either Italian or Jewish, so when I was sent to the grocery store I had to remember my Ps and Qs, to keep my demeanor respectful, and to speak politely to a white person, "No, Sir. Yes, Sir." And "No, Ma'am, Yes, Ma'am."

The rules were even more important when a trip was made to downtown Birmingham, a trip that we often made by bus.

Buses were strictly segregated, and this was imposed in several ways. When the bus pulled up, Black folk entered the bus by the front door, bought a ticket, exited, then walked to the door at the rear of the bus and climbed back aboard. Their place was behind the wooden sign which said "Colored" on one side and "White" on the other, which was moved to meet the needs of the white passengers. Black folk were not allowed in front of the infamous sign for any reason—even to stand. Body contact was also not permitted.

This made much of downtown Birmingham inaccessible to me, Leon and our father. In the white business area, Blacks were not welcome. However, there were exceptions dictated by economics; restaurants sometimes had a side window where Blacks could buy food. Then there were the theaters where Black folk could buy their ticket at the box office and then go around the corner to a side entrance and up to the balcony. The alley behind the theater smelled like a toilet because there was no toilet for Blacks in a white theater

Fourth Avenue was the area where I was headed with Leon and my father on a Saturday morning, a thriving area of Black businesses including restaurants, beauty shops, real estate offices and barbershops.

Picture a morning when we get off the bus on Fourth; the place is bustling; there are more men than women on the sidewalks and, like my father, who takes great care with his appearance, they're dressed in suits, dress shirts and ties. Most are wearing fedoras. The women wear dresses and small hats, purses on one arm, and shopping bags on the other.

As we wait for the traffic light to change, with our father firmly holding our hands, a trolley clangs past on the center rails of the street.

There's the sound of a horn from a shiny, black car and someone waves to our dad.

"That's a 1939 Chevy," he says, pointing out a shiny car with approval. He doesn't like Fords.

We make our way down the sidewalk to the barbershop.

As we walk in with our dad, the warm smell of hair tonic and aftershave fills my nose. Near the entrance, there are chairs for waiting customers; some are smoking and there's a selection of Black magazines including Jet and Ebony, plus Look and Life, on a table in front. A row of barber chairs on one side of the business faces four or five chairs on the other side for the shoeshine boys. It's a lively, cheerful place as the men talk about conditions in the city, the police, going fishing, and the Birmingham Black Barons. I am all ears as I watch the shoeshine boys snap their cloths as they work, polishing customers' shoes quickly and methodically—until they can see their faces in them. Then it's my turn for a haircut. The chair is pumped up with a whoosh of air, a booster seat added, and I'm lifted onto it. Tying an apron around my neck, the barber begins to clip.

"This boy takes a good haircut," the barber pronounces, as he finishes up.

While my father gets his shoes polished for church the next day, Leon and I get sodas from the ice cooler in the corner; 5 cents a soda with a two-cent deposit on the returned bottle.

Then there's a final stop before the journey home to Famous Dry Cleaners for Dad's white dress shirts that he always wears to work.

— 2 —

North to Chicago

Soon after the incident with the white police officer, at midnight, under the cover of darkness, our family boarded a train and joined the thousands of Blacks who moved from the South to the Windy City in the 1940's.

As we boarded the train, a Black Pullman porter directed our family to the segregated Jim Crow car for the journey north. On that first night of the journey, two little boys experienced for the first time the noise and excitement of train travel; the whistles, the clanging, and the hissing of steam as the big locomotive rumbled out of the station on the way to Chicago.

In the morning the porter came through the Jim Crow car tinkling a little bell, indicating that the white passengers had finished eating, and Black folk could now make their way to the dining room through the sleeping cars of the white passengers, along the narrow corridor that ran past their closed doors, backing away carefully from any passengers who came out of their compartments. In the dining room, I remember coffee stains on the white tablecloths that marked the place settings of the white diners who had eaten before us.

After breakfast, and back in our seats, there was not long to wait before the train pulled in to Chicago's bustling, noisy Union Station with its marble floors, soaring ceilings and windows letting in shafts of sunlight.

After our weary family disembarked on the railway platform, my father found a pay phone and placed the five cent call to a contact person. We huddled and waited. After an hour a man showed up with a car and transported us to a Black rooming house on Wabash Street, where we stayed for several days.

Every day, my father went out searching for a job. After three days he found his first job handling cattle in a stockyard. That allowed him to move our family into a "kitchenette" which consisted of a living room, with the use of a communal kitchen and a communal bathroom.

Life in Chicago brought an important new beginning in my life. At the age of six—soon to be seven—I attended school for the first time at Burke Elementary on Indiana Street and was placed in first grade because of my age. In the classroom, I recall only two things that I really liked: 2% sweet milk with cream on top and violin lessons. I tucked the violin under my chin, drew the bow, and liked the sound it made. Every day, Mr. Schoenenburger's voice reminded me, "Albert. 'C' note!"

Our family lived on Indiana Street long enough that I got to know and enjoy the neighborhood. One of my favorite times of the day was when the milkman drove his horse-drawn wagon into the alley every morning like clockwork. By six o'clock, I was outside waiting for the clip-clop of hooves on the cobblestones of the alley, shivering with cold and excitement.

The milkman's bay horse halted at the first stop, the milkman climbed down from the cab of his wagon with a milk carrier holding eight quarts of milk, and either placed the bottle of milk with a clink on a door stoop or into a milk chute, which was a small cupboard built into the wall of a house. Deliveries made, the milkman stepped back on board, the horse walked on several doors to the next stop and halted automatically. One day, I reached out to pet the milkman's horse, but it didn't pause to let me. The horse simply plodded on, then on out of the alley, water dripping from the melting blocks of ice inside the wagon onto the cobblestones.

When my father got a job as a fireman on the railway, our family moved for the third and last time in to another home; a somewhat unusual home in the back of a storefront church at 4756 Langley. Our living area was again a kitchenette, with beds, couch, kitchen table, and gas stove all in one living area, and an inside bathroom with a tub. On Sundays the entire church congregation shared our bathroom.

My dad was a member of the church and, in time, became a deacon. He cleaned and set up the church for Sunday mornings and our whole family attended services. The music of the church was gospel and one visiting singer was none other than the great Mahalia Jackson, the Queen of Gospel! I remember her singing "What a Friend You Have in Jesus" in her powerful voice. After church, Mahalia joined our family at our kitchen table for dinner. Leon and I used our best table manners.

Mahalia Jackson. (Carl Van Vechten Photographs collection at the Library of Congress.)

The move to the church on Langley Street meant I had to transfer to Forestfield Elementary, where it was discovered that I had never finished first grade, and in addition, had never even attended kindergarten. Disastrously, I was placed in kindergarten at age eight. I was too big for the class, and I cringed at the games I was expected to play. When kindergarten didn't work out, it was back into first grade, where I disliked intensely Dick and Jane, Baby Sally and Puff the Dog in the agonizingly boring books known to many first graders. I learned to read by sight, and to this day I have a wonderful memory but never learned phonics and could not sound out words. In my on-again, off-again schooling, I had even missed learning my ABC's.

Most distressing, I had a speech impediment that was to plague me for much of my life. I stuttered over the first word of anything that I was required to read or say out loud. It embarrassed and terrified me, and it seemed to me that my teachers thought I was a big, dumb boy. I never really stopped to consider that I was making greater strides than the previous generation in my family, because neither my father nor his parents ever learned to read or write. (I was also dyslexic, but did not understand the implications of this for many years.)

However, despite my difficulties with reading, life in first grade improved. The kids were friendlier than at my previous school, although there were scary females to contend with, including, to my horror, a white girl who tried to kiss me in the cloakroom where students left their galoshes. This situation absolutely terrified me. In Jim Crow South, having a white girl kiss you could put your life in danger.

When I started second grade, it was harder, but I did well in many things. I had my multiplication tables memorized, and arithmetic came easy for me. I really just needed help in reading. At home, Ella Bea—my stepmother—had no patience in helping me. She called me "dumb" and told me that I couldn't speak because "your tongue is too thick." Trying to get the sounds out and listening to her increasingly abusive words, I grew scared of her. She was mean. My father couldn't help with school work; indeed, it was Ella Bea who had taught my father to sign his name, in what could barely pass as legible cursive.

Things may have been difficult at school, but in other ways, life in Chicago was good. No one harassed me in the Chicago neighborhood. The streets were safe. Police were not to be feared as they were in Birmingham, and Leon and I often talked to the policemen sitting in their car in an alley as they tried to catch folks running numbers. In Chicago, Leon and I enjoyed doing many things together as brothers: playing in the alley or in front of the church, sledding in the snow, which was new to us, and still going to Western movies. I even remember the first time I watched TV. I stood outside a neighborhood store window in a small crowd, intently watching the test pattern of lines and symbols occasionally change to a number, on a machine that I was told was a "television."

It wasn't all play in Chicago. I held down two jobs on weekends: hauling groceries home from the local A&P grocery store in my red wagon and working in the local Laundromat. I could earn a quarter a trip hauling groceries home for customers, but older boys gave me a lot of competition, whereas the Laundromat brought in a dollar a day—quite a step up from the grocery stint! At the Laundromat, I took the clothes out of the washing machine into a basket, washed lint out of the filters in a bucket of water, and wheeled the clothes down to the dryers. I also swept the floor.

Albert Senior was still the Best of Dads. He took Leon and me to the park with our big German sheepdog, Jerry, and often took us fishing on Lake Michigan—a lake so big that it looked like an ocean to me. We sat on giant granite blocks on the side of the lake, and when my father cast his drag line with many hooks, he whirled it around his head like a lasso. (Little did I know that on the other side of the lake in Detroit, Michigan lived my biological mother. She would not come back into my life until many years later.)

On one special occasion, Albert Senior took Leon and me to the railway yard where he worked. It seemed like hundreds of railway tracks ran through the enormous yard, and big black locomotives belched out steam, both scary and fascinating to us. My dad lifted us up into the cab of a train and explained how it ran, and how he stoked the firebox. Then we climbed down and walked to the round house and saw a big locomotive being disconnected and turned to run in a new direction.

My father held his job at the railway for some years until the day he slipped on grease in the cab of his train, fell off, and hit his head. It was a serious fall. I remember the big egg-shaped lump on my father's head and the bandages binding the wound. Dad never returned to his job. There was no health care associated with his job, no sick days, and no worker's compensation.

Somehow or other, Mr. Poole in Birmingham learned of what was happening to us. He contacted Albert Senior and asked if he would ferry a new fleet of Cadillac hearses from Chicago to Birmingham. It meant lots of time away from home, but my father needed the work and took the job that would last for months, making the long drive from Chicago to Birmingham and then the return train trip north about six times.

Meanwhile, I did not pass second grade. Whether this contributed to Ella Bea's disintegration into the evil stepmother of legends, or the absence of my father was the main factor, she lost control when it came to punishing Leon and me. Several times, when my father was out of town, she beat us on our legs and backs with an ironing cord, leaving welts and warning us, "Don't tell your daddy!"

We didn't tell. Not for the time being.

However, we were not to remain in Chicago much longer. While my father was in Birmingham during his final trip, Mr. Poole offered him his old job back. It had been five years. It was safe to return home to the South.

— 3 —
Back Down South

Driving while Black, or DWB, is a hazardous occupation, even today, in this country. Blacks are pulled over in disparate numbers since there is a presumption of guilt based on racial profiling which can lead to arrest and incarceration. Just ask a Black male to tell you of his experiences on our highways. In the 1940's, the situation was much more dangerous than it is today as my father, stepmother, Leon and I drove to Alabama with a Black minister who was heading south.

The route was paved with hazards. The northern states were less dangerous in general, but below the Mason-Dixon line it was particularly fraught when drivers went through Indiana into Tennessee—Klan territory. Regardless of whether it was a northern or southern state, the basic rules were the same: carry your food with you, plan your trip from gas station to gas station and then drive straight through.

Once Blacks crossed the Mason-Dixon line, the law changed, which raised the risk involved for Black travelers like us. There were no hotels for Black people, no restaurants to stop in, and no bathrooms for Blacks other than in bus stations or train stations. (People went behind bushes, alongside the road and in the woods, as fast as possible so the cops didn't catch them.) Black drivers slowed down a lot going through towns, and they kept to the main highways. Some towns had "sunset laws" that meant Black people would be arrested for just being in town after the sun went down. I soaked all of this in, and it had a deep effect on my life.

I remember that sometimes at a gas station you could buy a pop from an outside ice-box, drink it and either leave the bottle, or pay the deposit. But, every time Black drivers stopped at a gas station, they took a chance. And if you did encounter a white person, you had to "know your place." Don't look them in the eye. Turn your head and look down. Say, "Yes, Sir," and "No, Sir." Act like you are stupid or dumb. Follow these rules just to be left alone, to survive.

Thankfully, our family reached Birmingham safely and were dropped off with our suitcases at Poole's Funeral Chapels.

Mr. Poole was to pay my dad over $20 a week for work as funeral director, ambulance driver and embalmer. With that income and Ella Bea's salary as a nurse (which was greater), our family could live quite well. We secured a decent home in the segregated Black housing of Birmingham—the best house that we had lived in to date; a single-level four-plex in the projects made of cinder block. Every house had a front yard and a back yard. Inside, the home had two bedrooms, a living-room, kitchen, and an inside bathroom. My dad was able to buy furniture and a Frigidaire with a tiny freezer that held two ice trays. Leon and I were fascinated by the light that came on and off with the opening and closing of the fridge door.

I was enrolled in school and placed in 3rd grade. My teacher, Mrs. Tigg was a light-skinned Black woman with long, dark hair who wore gold-rimmed glasses and pretty dresses. I remember her as kind, and it made me happy that she liked me. Mrs. Tigg had also lived in Chicago, and she would tell the kids in my classroom about all the things that you could do in that northern city: riding the L train, going to the Chicago Zoo where the great gorilla, Bushman, lived, and about the five Great Lakes and the largest of those lakes, Lake Michigan.

I got some reflected glory for having lived in Chicago too.

Every Friday was a spelling bee. Girls stood in front of the chalk-board, and boys stood opposite, in front of the windows, as they spelled out their words. But I always made sure that I couldn't participate and endure the misery of trying to get the first sound out by refusing to study for the spelling bee.

Despite the handicap of my stutter, I thrived in Mrs. Tigg's class. I did well in arithmetic, writing and in cursive, where I got top marks. I was made the board monitor and was proud of the fact that I washed the chalkboard better than anyone else. The other boys were jealous. In art, I loved drawing and drew on the board for Mrs. Tigg. In history, another of my favorite subjects, I remember in detail a drawing that I made of the Boston Tea Party with the ship, men dressed like Indians, and boxes of tea floating in the harbor.

Mrs. Tigg wanted her students to be able to get up and speak in front of their classmates about their future goals. Despite my difficulties in speech, I voiced my desire to be a doctor or a lawyer to the class.

As Leon and I got older, we were expected to do more chores at home. I washed the dishes, and Leon dried. Every evening the cabinets had to be washed down and the floor swept. Now, at the age of nine, soon to be ten, I was beginning to cook. Although cooking opened some innate talents in me that blossomed over the years, one of my early cooking experiments did not turn out too well. I wanted to surprise my stepmother and make biscuits and a hoke cake for my father. They were beautiful; they had risen high and baked a golden brown. Ella Bea showed them proudly to a neighbor, and I enjoyed her approval until we sat down to eat. Yuck! The biscuits tasted like Alka-Seltzer. I had used baking soda instead of baking powder and apparently used way too much of it!

Far from gaining the approval of our stepmother, Leon and I increasingly earned her anger, and she turned on us with a vengeance. I was used to exacting standards in doing chores, but now I was expected to do extensive housework in a meticulous fashion. In the kitchen, the cabinets, floor, and stove top had to be spotlessly clean every evening. When Ella Bea found the smallest fault, she turned into an evil and vindictive person.

In his work as an ambulance driver, my father was gone every other night, and on those evenings all hell could break loose. When rage consumed her, Ella Bea screamed the order, "Get in to the bedroom!"

My stomach in knots, I would tell myself, "This is going to hurt," but I feared her and obeyed her.

Our stepmother would tie first me and then Leon, both of us whimpering, to the bedpost and beat us unmercifully on our backs and arms with an electrical cord, and after the beating, as we sobbed, always the command, "Don't tell your father!"

In the mix of what went wrong in the Wilkerson family, were the men who came to the house, one at a time, always when our father was gone. They came for penicillin shots—medicine that was stored in the refrigerator. After giving the shot, Ella Bea often sat at the kitchen table talking to her patient. One evening, I remember a man came into the house wearing a gun. He claimed he was a Secret Service agent. Ella Bea told him to take the gun out of his holster while she gave the shot. He did so and laid it on the table. Suddenly, there was a knock at the door.

"Who is it?" called out Ella Bea.

"Daddy!" came the answer.

The "Secret Service" man sprang up, grabbed his gun and ran out the back door!

———— • ————

Finally, the physical abuse that had started in Chicago came to an end. Ella Bea had been careless about where she administered her punishment, and the welts from the electrical cord showed on Leon and me, below our shirt sleeves. Our father asked what the marks were, and finally, we told our father about the beatings. The next thing I knew, Leon and I were whisked out the door by our dad. It was to be the end of living in a family setting with our father and stepmother.

Tough times lay ahead.

— 4 —

One Summer

That summer, after telling our Dad about the whippings from Ella Bea, we left our home in the projects and were virtually homeless. In the way of misfortunes never coming singly, our father had been laid off from Poole's, and without our stepmother's income, we were in extreme financial straits. There were no unemployment benefits, nor compensation of any kind for my dad to lean on. He picked up work at various Black funeral homes: embalming, building coffins, driving an ambulance or directing a funeral. But where to stay presented a big problem. We could not afford another home and slept wherever we could lay down our heads: in a borrowed car, on the front porch of a house, or the porch of a funeral home.

Eventually, a better solution presented itself when my father took us over to his brother, JD, out in the country. James Daniel was his name, but everyone called him JD. He was in the process of building his own house, and he needed extra hands. The outside of the house was constructed of the rough exterior slabs of wood cut from tree trunks that JD hauled from the sawmill. Leon and I made ourselves useful, carrying lumber and hammering in nails.

Everything went well with JD and his wife Mattie until Leon and I got up one morning feeling very hungry to find ourselves in an empty house. Instead of going out to the nearby fields and woods, to pick mulberries or wild plums, which we had previously done, we peeked in the pantry. Among the supplies were several cans of peas. We debated. Would Aunt Mattie miss one? We took a chance, opened a can and split the contents.

Mattie was furious, and we were immediately no longer welcome there.

After some nights sleeping in a 1936 green Chevy coupe, my father took us to his older brother Levy's house where we could sleep on the couch.

It was made clear to Leon and me that we had to work for our keep, and to avoid getting evicted from another uncle's house, Leon and I began "dumpster-diving" to deal with our hunger and to bring home food to Uncle Levy's house. We pulled a handmade wooden cart to the Farmer's Market, held on a big vacant lot near the railway tracks on Thursday, Friday, and Saturday. We had to be there at 5 a.m. sharp when the vendors began setting up their stalls. It was a noisy, bustling place with trucks driving in and out, horse drawn carts rumbling in, and trains rattling past.

Our wagon was set up for transporting food home to Uncle Levy's house. Wax paper was spread in the wagon and glass containers were ready for smaller items.

Digging in the dumpsters was demonstrated by Uncle Levy. One of our most important jobs was to push aside the top layers of fish heads on which flies were gathering, pick out fresh fish heads and load them in to the wagon. The big heads of red snapper were the best.

All the vendors were white. A few got angry and tried to chase us away, but we quickly learned to avoid them. Most vendors accepted the presence of the two little Black boys who scavenged in an orderly way, because we always cleaned up any mess we made. In addition to fish heads, we searched for edible fruit and vegetables in the garbage cans beside stalls. (I carried a little pocket knife to cut off the rotten parts.) Desirable vegetables included intact pea pods. I remember a little, old, white lady who, seeing us coming, grasped a handful of fresh pea pods, laying them on top of the discarded vegetable scraps, and then turned her head away as we picked them up.

On the days that we went to the Farmer's Market, we ate our breakfast there. One day, we hit a bonanza! We had been getting ready to leave when I noticed a big transfer truck loaded with watermelons.

"Leon," I said, "That man can't drive that truck!"

The driver was jerking and crashing through the gears, jostling the vehicle. As we watched, one watermelon rolled off the truck and dropped to the ground. Quick on our feet, we darted to the rear of the truck. Another watermelon started to roll. Leon spread his arms wide and the melon dropped into his arms—such a whopper that it knocked him clean to the ground!

Leon and I sat and ate watermelon until we were stuffed.

———◆———

In addition to dumpster diving, we had many other duties. We resumed housework—cleaning the kitchen and mopping the floors. Outside we swept the hard dirt backyard, and in front of the house, kept the tiny plot of grass trimmed by clipping the grass with a pair of household scissors.

Wednesday was laundry day—a big work day. We washed clothes for the household, an operation involving three big tubs of water—one to scrub the clothes using a bar of brown soap and a washboard, and two tubs of rinse water. There was also a kettle of boiling water for the white stuff, and an extra rinse for the whites with bluing. Once we got the clothes through the wash "cycle" and rinsed, the clothes had to be well wrung out until our hands ached, and then hung on the wire clothesline with clothespins.

After we were done, the tubs of rinse water were used for baths.

Despite all the work at our uncle's house, there were benefits to living there. I liked my Aunt Hattie. She was nice. She also had a stutter, which made me feel comfortable, and, in addition, she was a good cook. She made delicious pancakes and there was nothing so fine in the morning as hearing Hattie call, "C'mon boys and get my gold medal pancakes!"

Uncle Levy was a hard worker and an entrepreneur. His main job was working as an armed night guard at Famous Dry Cleaners—the Black laundry facility on Fourth Avenue. After his shift, Levy came home in the morning and slept until around 11 a.m., when his customers began to appear. He was a barber, plying his trade on the front porch of the house. Friday and Saturday were his busiest days. In addition to cutting hair, he made ice cream in the ice cube trays of the refrigerator. Homemade ice cream and 50 cent shots of whiskey were dispensed to customers from either the porch or the side door of the house.

———— ♦ ————

It had been a good summer, but our visit came to an end. We had worked hard, been safe and cared for and learned a lot about surviving.

— 5 —

So-Mo Food

At the end of the summer spent with Uncle Levy, Albert Senior went into business with a friend, Robert Merriweather, making caskets. Steel caskets were becoming popular, and to meet the demand my father and Robert produced both steel and wooden ones. The change affected Leon and me; we were again living in our own house, but it was in a business area, and there were few kids to play with.

For some reason, I do not remember a lot about the school I attended that year at Woodlawn Elementary, other than that all the teachers were Black and one male teacher showed my favorite western movies at lunchtime. The films ran about 30 minutes and sometimes were part of a series, so the kids got to look forward to the next one.

———◆———

Unfortunately, the casket-making business floundered after about nine months. My father was again unemployed and had to leave us for three days as he went looking for a job. There was enough food in the house to last—but being boys, we ate everything in a couple of days and woke up on the third day to empty shelves and feeling very hungry.

The answer was in our garbage. Leon and I retrieved the potato peelings that had been discarded the night before, washed them carefully and then dried them to prevent spattering. Then we built a fire on the ground in the small, dirt back yard and using a long-handled camp-style frying pan fried the potato peelings in bacon drippings. We hunkered down waiting for the potatoes to cook, stomachs turning

24

over with anticipation and hunger and our mouths watering. When it was finally ready, we topped off the dish with hot sauce and ate with abandon.

Later in the day, our father arrived home with a bag of groceries.

————◆————

Luckily, Poole's Funeral Chapels had expanded, and my father got his job back with the company. This meant a return to the projects for our family—back to a friendly neighborhood and kids to play with.

Schools for Blacks were not in the neighborhood where we lived, and there were no school buses. Lewis School was a good 45-minute walk from home for Leon and me. In Birmingham, under Jim Crow law, Black schools (and Black Codes in general) were for anyone who was even part Black. At Lewis School, a girl named Dorothy attended, and I remember how she stuck out with her golden braids and white skin.

Lewis School was a "passing" school, which meant I had different teachers for different subjects. Two teachers who were particularly sharp and professional were Miss. Bueller and Miss. Holloway. Miss. Bueller taught Social Studies and English. She had ivory skin with a hint of brown and long, brown hair. She dressed nicely and always wore stockings, although I remember the hair on her legs showing through! Miss. Holloway taught music, which included piano and choir, the choir comprised of the entire fifth grade. I liked her but didn't look forward to her rapping me on the knuckles for some infraction or other.

Summer school at Lewis was for enrichment and to prepare boys and girls for the next year of school, and both Leon and I attended because there really wasn't anything else to do. There were classes in history, poetry and art and crafts. I was good at art and enjoyed making things. I built model soapbox cars and baskets made from Popsicle sticks or strips of construction paper. One creative project transformed 78 records into bowls by dipping them into hot water to soften them and then pulling them out of the water via a string looped through the hole in the center. Most of the art projects involved repurposing or recycling materials rather than using expensive art supplies, since Black schools didn't have a budget for canvases and paint. At the time, we were not aware of this discrepancy and found joy in the materials at hand. Students worked at various tables, and I was made assistant to the teacher and walked round the classroom helping and giving advice.

Our dad furnished our modest home with beds for himself and each of us, a couch and a big chair in the living room. A coffee table was put together from concrete blocks and a glass top, and our dad made a table and chairs for the kitchen. I contributed by making a lamp for the living room, assembled from parts I scavenged from the trash including a base made from a glass fixture. I stripped wires, screwed things together using a butter knife as a screwdriver, and nervously plugged it in when I was finished. Would it work? Yes! The lamp came on.

At the age of eleven, my main duties were taking care of Leon and cooking the evening meal for three. In the kitchen was a gas stove with a cook top and a double oven. However, when money was especially tight, the gas was turned off, and I cooked the evening meal on a single electrical hot plate. Every night for four months, I made black-eyed peas flavored with pork-rind and salt and pepper in a big aluminum pot. The peas needed to be simmered on low throughout the day, and I had to stay nearby to make sure they didn't burn.

The food budget was less than a dollar per day for all three of us, and every cent counted. Black-eyed peas cost 10 cents a bag, and I used a half bag per day. Included in the budget were milk, a loaf of bread, and 15 cents worth of bologna. On a good week, we had other items on hand, and I cooked fresh green beans made with potatoes and pig skins. Lima beans, red beans and rice (bulk rice cost 10 cents a bag) rounded out our diet.

Occasionally Leon and I found delicious tomatoes growing wild.

I became a master at making hot water cornbread. I mixed corn meal, white flour, salt and baking soda together and added bacon fat.

This went into a frying pan on the hot plate. When bubbles rose to the top of the mixture, I flipped it over and browned the other side.

No one in those times talked about "soul food"—it was survival food, and it was a struggle to keep our bellies full. That's why I coined the phrase "so-mo food"—short for "some more food."

Luckily there were some interesting ways for us to stretch our diet.

Not far over the railroad tracks were fields, then low rising hills, and finally woods of yellow pine where, in season, Leon and I picked blackberries, raspberries, and gathered crab apples and black walnuts from trees. Picking walnuts and smashing the hard shells between rocks to get to the nut was fun. Muscadines grew there also—a purple-black type of grape, tart, and juicy. I remember the taste as I would pop one into my mouth, chew up the soft flesh and spit out the seeds.

Most importantly, the fields and woods brought a sense of freedom and peace to me. Walking there, enjoying the rural setting, gathering fruit and nuts was something that my dad had introduced us to, and for all of my life I have associated nature with my father.

We found the greatest fun gathering up peanuts. Every third day a train pulling freight cars loaded with peanuts rumbled by on the railway tracks near the projects. The rattling of the train shook loose peanuts from the open cars, and a steady trickle of nuts fell to the tracks, as Leon and I discovered happily. We started following the trains, walking along and chomping down as many peanuts as possible.

Weekends and evenings were the times for playing outside with the neighborhood kids. In addition to games, there was the added excitement of watching television regularly, for the first time in my life. A neighbor in our court bought a 12-inch screen television (black and white of course). These neighbors lived about four doors down. Every Wednesday night, about ten kids showed up for "I Love Lucy." The first lucky five got to sit on the floor in front of the set, and the rest watched through the screen door. Sometimes we even got snacks.

Right after "Lucy," Leon and I put on our own show on the porch outside, with the kids who had gathered to watch TV as our audience.

Our comedy routine, headlining Leon as the comedian and me as the serious guy, replayed the funniest skits from that evening's show or acted out the repartee of other famous duos such as Dean Martin and Jerry Lewis or Amos and Andy. The neighborhood kids cracked up, and we loved the attention.

Besides taking care of Leon, cooking, going to school, and entertaining other kids with our homemade comedy skits, I had a responsible weekend job. I babysat five babies, all around seven or eight months, in the U-shaped courtyard in front of our home. I pushed the babies back and forth in their strollers, fed them a bottle when they wanted one, and sang "Rock-a-bye Baby" to them. Thankfully they slept in the sunshine most of the time! My favorite baby was Milk and Gristles—I named her this, because she liked milk and her bones felt soft.

———◆———

Leon and I were happily settled into our routine, but little did we know that another move was already in the works. At last, Albert Senior fulfilled a dream and went in to business for himself. Our family moved to Seventh Avenue into a large wooden building on a corner. My father's business was in the front and our living area in the rear. My dad painted the entire building white. One side read "Wilkerson and Sons Casket Company" in big, black letters, for all to see.

There was a telephone for the business—the first phone in our family, but no vehicle for transporting caskets. Customers either picked up a casket or my dad borrowed a truck. Two employees worked for him. One employee, Miss. Elizabeth, cooked dinner for the family in addition to sewing the silk linings for caskets.

As part of the family business, Leon and I helped in every way we could: stacking lumber, picking up nails and sweeping up wood for burning, dusting and cleaning. My dad made his own wood glue, so heat and hot water was constantly needed.

One big family lived nearby—so big that they lived in both units of a duplex. Leon and I thought that family was rich because they

28

occupied such a large space, and that family thought the same of us because we owned a business.

In our new neighborhood, there were few kids around in our age group. Leon and I often had to make our own entertainment. Luckily, there was a swimming hole in a creek nearby, and in the summer, we met up with other boys at "The Waterfall" to swim. The rule was that you swam nude unless you had pubic hair—then you had to wear a swimsuit.

——————— ♦ ———————

In addition to his own casket-making shop, my dad continued to take extra jobs as a funeral director. Indeed, things went so well that he bought his first car; a 1941 sky-blue Oldsmobile. We nicknamed the car Blue Goose, and it carried us on several camping trips. Soon, we got new clothes, including the powder blue suits we wore one Easter Sunday, along with shoes, shirts, and sharp haircuts.

As always, my dad got us up for school each morning. He often woke us with a song he made up:

"Get up and pee on the rock

It ain't quite day

But it's five o'clock."

We would stumble out of bed to the smell of coffee percolating and fried sweet potatoes and eggs. We ate, cleaned up the dishes, and were out of the door by 6:45 for the walk to school, Leon with a biscuit sandwich for later.

After about a year, the economy slacked off and Albert Senior was forced to close the business. We lost the building and with it our home. Again, we needed a place to live and moved up the road to a big rooming house at 805 North 8th Street. We stayed in the last room on the right in the rear. My father was back at Poole's.

By this time, I was 13. I got a job, across from Poole's, in a grocery store owned by an Italian family. It was the only grocery store in the all-Black neighborhood and was open every day. On Sundays, however, because of the Blue Laws, only part of the store opened, sectioned off from the main store by a curtain. Candy and a few canned goods were sold on that day, but no meat, butter, vegetables or beer could be sold.

I cleaned up, took out the trash, and stacked shelves for a dollar a day. I also carried home groceries for ladies who usually tipped me five or ten cents.

There was an older kid, Dexter, who was 16 years old, working for the Italian family too. Unfortunately for Dexter, he had not gotten very far in school, and he wasn't very smart, so when Dexter got sick and I took over his job, it became a permanent arrangement. Now I helped wait on customers, filling orders, and bringing canned goods and other items to the counter.

The Italian family had a girl and a boy, named Charles, who was 10. Every morning Charles ate Corn Flakes with coffee, milk and sugar. He was a short, ratty-faced boy with pale skin, and big ears, and he was full of his own importance. Charles informed me in a snotty voice that I should say "Yes, Sir" when I spoke to him; however, his mother overheard.

"Charles. You're not talking to Dexter," Miss. Rose cautioned him, and ended the pipsqueak's attempt to lord it over me.

I remember always being hungry. Sometimes, the proprietor, Mr. Joe, gave me a treat—a cookie or half a sandwich. One day, Mr. Joe's family had chicken cacciatore for dinner, made of chicken, peppers, onions and tomatoes. My stomach ached with the smell. Maybe Mr. Joe realized how hungry I was; he told his wife to give me a plate, and when Miss. Rose finished eating, she spooned another serving on to her plate, without washing it, and handed me the chicken cacciatore along with her dirty fork.

Part of my upbringing was a dire warning to never eat at someone else's house, because you never knew if the family had clean habits. And now I was literally being handed a meal on someone's dirty plate along with a used fork! Hunger won out over scruples. I took the meal, left the kitchen (I was not allowed to eat in the same area as the family) and went to the back room of the store to eat the entire serving.

30

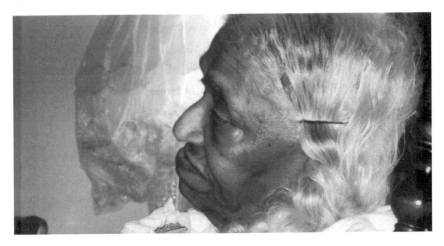

Albert's Mom, Grace, in her 80's.

On a Friday or Saturday, I was taking a break outside the store, sitting on a milk crate on the sidewalk. It was nearly midday, and the street was quiet. A taxi pulled up from the direction of downtown, and the passenger-side door opened. As I watched, a tall lady stepped out of the taxi. She had long hair and was wearing a smart gray suit in a houndstooth pattern. She walked a few steps closer to me.

"Is your name Albert Junior?" she asked.

"Yes," I replied, "How do you know my name?"

"I'm your mother, Grace."

"You are?"

"Yes. Do you know Leola?"

"Yes."

"Well. I'm her sister."

"Do we have a sister called Mary Catherine?" I asked, because I had been told this by my father, and when Grace nodded, asked, "Well, where is she?"

"We live in Detroit. I came to take you back there if you want to go."

My father had told us only that our mother and a sister, Mary Catherine, lived in Detroit, Michigan. Most other details had been

31

omitted, and he hadn't seemed too keen on talking about our mother in general. We knew that Leon's twin, Roy, had died as a baby, and we visited his grave once with our father. Other than some T-shirts that had been brought by Leola to our home from our mother, there had been no discussion of life with her, and no contact with her. I had absolutely no memory of my mother. Now here was this tall, well-dressed stranger, who said she was my mom, offering a new life in the North.

It sounded inviting.

— 6 —

In Detroit

On the Greyhound journey to Detroit, it was the back of the bus for our mother, Leon and me until the Mason-Dixon line was crossed. After that demarcation, we could change seats.

Early on, the next morning, we arrived in the downtown Detroit bus station. My mother's husband, Eddie, picked us up in a 1949 Mercury. "You see that car with the broken taillight? That's Eddie," said our mother.

Leon and I looked at each other when we saw him. Our first reaction was that Eddie was big, fat, and kind of ugly, and he was dressed differently than any other male that had been in our lives so far. To us, our mother with her sharp suit and Eddie in casual, untidy clothes made an odd couple.

We drove to the house on 1645 Gladstone Street. The home was a single-family residence and consisted of three bedrooms, a dining room, kitchen and a living room which was bare of furniture—but spotlessly clean like the rest of the house. There were four sisters in the family, all strangers to us. One sister was excited to see us; our biological, full sister, Mary Catherine, was light-skinned and pretty, and about nine or ten at the time. We ate and then went out to see our new surroundings. The neighborhood was attractive, tree-lined, with grass lawns in front of red-brick houses and two-family flats. On our walk we decided on a few things. We were going to call Eddie "Dad"—as opposed to "Daddy," which we called Albert Senior, and our mother, a more formal "Mother," since we didn't know her well.

———— ◆ ————

The school that I would attend was only half a block from the house. Hutcheson Intermediate. Leon was still in elementary that year, and it would be the first time that we attended different schools.

When the time came for school to start, I enrolled myself, and when school began I felt quite comfortable in my new setting, thanks to school in Chicago. Some things, however, made an initial impression on me: books were new instead of the much-used ones in Black schools in the South, there was a gymnasium with actual showers, and lunch was served in a cafeteria. It was a full course, hot meal served from steam tables. Unfortunately, the cooks were white, and, to me, the food was bland, tasteless "white food."

The school population at Hutcheson was integrated and was comprised of five percent Black, 75% Jewish (which was then regarded as a race) and 20% White. All the teachers were white, except one.

The 7th grade classes, in which I was placed, were hard, and the other students were ahead of me, but I quickly got involved, and the teachers liked me. As for the students, they were OK. In my first year, I had no male friends, but some of the girls were quite friendly.

Every morning began with swimming. Swimming nude with white boys was a new experience. Showers before swimming were mandatory and before entering the pool boys had to bend over and spread their cheeks for inspection. I loved swimming, and in the evening after school, I often returned to the pool with Leon.

The teachers were fine, and I got along with them, but I did not like the boys' principal; he was mean to Black students and gave me a bad feeling. Later, when I was graduating from Hutcheson, that same principal would deprive me of my dream of going to Detroit's best high school.

Home room was with Miss. Cooper on the second floor, while her twin sister taught right above her on the third. Miss. Cooper was a white lady in her forties with gray hair. One day she pulled me aside.

Albert's sister, Mary Catherine, visiting in 2018.

"Albert," she said quietly. "Would you like to know something?"

"Yes, Ma'am," I answered, politely.

"Do you see my hair? I use grease on my hair."

Miss. Cooper's somewhat peculiar revelation was an attempt to relate to me. She was using Royal Crown hair dressing that was commonly used in the Black community. I wasn't sure what to say or how to react, so I just listened nervously and was polite.

———————◆———————

As Leon and I integrated into life with my mother and girl siblings, it seemed as though our young sisters were always fussing or crying. It was irksome and new. No one ever asked about our lives in Birmingham with our father—including our mother and Catherine, who had the same father as me and Leon. At the back of both of our minds were our father's words telling us that if things didn't work out, we should telephone him at Poole's.

"I'll get you back here," he had told us.

In the early days of coming to Detroit, our mother, Grace, took us round to the white side of the family that originated from our grandfather. As an attempt at bridging the ethnic divide, it was a failure. The first cousins were standoffish and didn't interact in any way with Leon or me.

35

Decades later, Albert and his sister, Gracie, visiting Detroit in front of an apple tree that helped feed them during difficult days when they were young.

But some things were good. Our mother cooked supper every night, and we ate more than we ever had. When my 14th birthday rolled around in October, I was asked what I would like to eat, and at my request my mother prepared a meal of fried chicken and a lemon sheet cake with chocolate icing. It was the first time that I had ever had a birthday cake.

Chores at home included taking the trash out with Leon and sweeping off the front porch. In the morning we had to go down to the basement and light the hot-water heater. Most importantly in the winter, we were made responsible for keeping the furnace in the basement stoked, shoveling coal out of the small room where it had been dumped via the coal chute, and keeping up the steam for the silver-painted radiators that heated the house (the temperature gauge on the furnace had to be kept within a certain range to accomplish this). We also had to clean the ashes out of the furnace. All of this brought to our minds our father's job as fireman on the railroads of Chicago.

Both myself and Leon tried to stay out of the house and away from our crying little sisters as much as possible. After school we were either at the school playground, in the pool, or at some other school activity. White kids just didn't appear on the streets, and our family was the only

Black family in the neighborhood, a neighborhood made up of Jewish families on one side of the street and on the other side, Germans.

In time, I became accepted by both Jews and Germans.

When I entered eighth grade, I got the only Black, male teacher in Detroit for metal shop—a class that I really enjoyed, just as I had enjoyed wood shop the previous year. In metal shop, I learned blacksmithing: bending, forging, and pounding metal. I excelled in the class, and the teacher acknowledged this by saying, "You seem to catch on better than the rest of the boys. You go round and help the others, and I'll give you a "B."

So, I made my way around the class, making sure the other boys were safe, supervising how the hot metal objects were taken from the gas furnace and placed in the concrete sand bin, and sand poured over them to cool, as my teacher sat behind his desk drinking coffee.

By the time that I was ready to leave Hutcheson Intermediate, I had determined I wanted to attend Cass High School. It was the best high school in Detroit. I needed a "B" average and had that. However, I also needed the recommendation of the boys' principal. When I asked him for this, instead of giving me a glowing endorsement, the principal said, "You people do better with your hands and you're going to vocational school."

As far as I know, no Black students were recommended to Cass by this principal. Ironically, a Black PhD who now lives in San Diego, and who attended Hutcheson, was also denied. He later was invited to Detroit as an educational consultant.

The next best high school was Central. To be eligible, I enrolled in three extra academic classes in summer school. One of those classes was an enrichment class that stressed how to use your brain effectively. It included exercises in writing, drawing, and listening to music, and it fascinated me.

Central High was in a rich, white neighborhood, about a 45-minute steady walk from home. It helped that I had two Black friends from Hutcheson attending Central High, too. Jessie was light-skinned and Windell played a sax—he was the only friend of mine who owned a car.

In class, desks were two-seaters. In one class, I sat beside Beverly. She was a pretty, mixed-race girl with long, brown hair, who scared me to death. One day she tried to hug me, and I fell off my chair onto the floor, trying to escape her. I told her to leave me alone, but she never did and continued to write endless notes and flirt with me any chance she got.

In two classes, a cute, curly-haired Jewish girl called Sheila was my seat-mate. She wore blouses and tweed skirts with bobby socks and saddle shoes. Sheila's locker was side-by-side with mine. One day when we were both at our lockers, Beverly stormed up.

"What are you doing talking to Albert?" she demanded of Sheila.

"We're friends in history and geography," replied Sheila, with a toss of her curls.

I was scared of both girls and made my escape as quickly as possible.

———— ◆ ————

During the summer break between Hutcheson Intermediate and Central High, I began working for a Jewish couple by the name of Spitzer in our neighborhood; they had a grocery store on 12th Street that sold kosher goods: cheese, hot dogs, pickled herring, smoked fish, Matzo meal, Manischewitz products and much more. It was a typical, small Jewish store of the time. Entering the front door, between two large-paned windows, customers walked up to the counter on the left where the large, brass, National Cash Register sat. Behind the counter, shelves were stacked high with cans and boxes. Further on down the counter was the section for making sandwiches out of meats and cheeses, and behind that counter, a big refrigerator, where soda pop and beer was stocked. The smell of salami, lox, and ground poppy seed was always in the air.

The Spitzers were an older couple. Mr. Spitzer's first name was Fritz. He wore glasses, had a bald head, large ears and wore an apron.

He was nice to me but always business-like, and he expected me to keep myself busy. Mrs. Spitzer was short, no more than five feet, stout, and wore glasses. She usually wore a dress with an apron tied around her substantial body.

My job was to stock shelves, clean, help customers and deliver groceries. Of course, I got tips when I delivered those groceries and realized that I could deliver more quickly and carry several orders at one time by bicycle. So, I saved up for a Schwinn bike, black with white pinstripes, and fitted it out with a basket. On weekdays, I worked from 3 to 7 p.m., but on Saturdays, the store's busiest day, I was in and out of Spitzer's all day long from 10 o'clock in the morning until 10 at night, peddling my bike as fast as I could from one customer's house to another.

Inside the store, one of my favorite tasks was dressing the windows, carefully stacking boxes and cans for display and rotating the goods once a week. When it came to marking the prices on cans, I took pride in my exact numbering—a skill that I had learned in my mechanical drawing class. My least favorite job was fishing out pickled herring from the back of the meat case, letting it drain, and then double wrapping it for the customer. It was disgustingly smelly.

The customers were practically all Jewish, other than a few Black customers, including a Black male who came in with his blonde, Jewish wife who he met in WWII. The Spitzers really approved of this couple, and sometimes I got to wait on them. Also, Leon occasionally came in with some girls, and a Black chef from the restaurant next door came in for beer. All the customers, regardless of ethnicity, treated me well. In addition, I was soon a favorite of Mrs. Spitzer and, when her husband got on to me, she would say, "Fritz. Leave the boy alone. He's a good worker," and when I was there at lunch time, "Albert. We're going to go have lunch," she'd say, and I would follow her up to the apartment above the store where she sometimes fed me Matzo ball soup, especially good on the cold, snowy days of a Detroit winter.

I watched how everything was done: the cutting of the cheese on the machine, and the cutting of salami by hand, carefully and uniformly.

39

One day, trying to impress Mrs. Spitzer, I decided to fill a customer's order for a quarter pound of salami, by myself. Mr. Spitzer was at the meat counter, ever alert; he called out when he saw me start slicing the meat, "Albert! What are you doing?" But, on inspection, my slicing was acceptable, and from then on, I could slice meat and cheese when the store got busy.

On yet another day, I used the big, manual cash register for the first time without being told to. Mr. Spitzer heard the "Brrng!" of the register and came over to check on me. Acknowledging that I might be ready to make sales, Mr. Spitzer proceeded to test me thoroughly on mental arithmetic. In time, when the store was busy, I did everything needed, including taking phone orders that were called in by customers.

The phoned-in orders included kosher bakery goods and vegetables that the Spitzers bought from other stores, and one of my favorite jobs was cycling over to Mr. Frank's bakery for bagels, onion rolls, Kaiser rolls or poppy seed rolls—my treat from Mr. Frank was a brownie or a butter horn—then on to Mr. Jack's for vegetables where I was told, "If you want a pickle you need to get it for yourself!"

I would roll up my sleeve and plunge my hand down into the big barrel of vinegary brine to pull out a kosher pickle.

———— ◆ ————

And so, now, I was doing well in school, at Spitzers, and at home, where things were relatively calm, but, as it goes for many of us, life would grow more complicated as my teenage years progressed—in fact, things became increasingly fractured.

— 7 —

Things Fall Apart

The thin, weasel-faced teacher in the white smock made his rounds of the drafting class, stopping to speak to most students, yet seldom speaking to the three Black boys in the class, including me. I had this teacher for both drafting and mechanical mathematics, classes that were important to me because—thinking ahead—I decided that I wanted to be a mechanical engineer. I was good in art, wood shop and metal shop and my overall grades were good, but the stumbling block was this teacher who was continually negative about my work. In drafting, for example, my arrows that I took pains over making so exactly, never seemed to satisfy the teacher. When I compared my work to others in the class, it seemed just as good or better. Most telling was the fact that I was never allowed to attend a career day and never recommended for a scholarship although my grades qualified.

Not only was school frustrating, but things were unraveling at home. Eddie was working two jobs—construction by day and another job at night—and my mother was not satisfied with one paycheck to run the household—she wanted two. This kept Eddie stretched thin and their relationship on edge. It was an expensive house to manage with a family of eight living there. And when family members started coming up from the South—endless cousins and aunts—looking for a temporary place to live until they got established in Detroit, extra food was needed and was produced at all hours in what seemed like an endless meal. It was always noisy at home, with kids crying and adults coming and going. It seemed like no one had any time for me.

41

Eddie got fed up with the situation. He started going out every Saturday night, refused to hand over his second paycheck to my mother, and the verbal fights that had started between them grew louder and more frequent.

As a partial solution to my discomfort at home, I wanted some independence, and a way to do that was earning more money. The biggest portion of my wages from Spitzer's was always turned over to my mother for the household. Often my wages were paid in kind, with food: staples like bread, milk and eggs. For me to have any money for myself, I had to get a second job.

Hazel's Chicken Shack served up roasted chicken, fried shrimp, barbeque spare ribs, and potato salad. Hazel, the owner, took me on for the 7:30 to 11 evening shift. I had half an hour to get from Spitzer's to Hazel's every evening. It didn't leave much time for homework, but, discouraged with school, I tried to get it done in my study hall period.

It was important to me that I looked good at both school and work, values that my father had impressed upon me. I washed the few changes of clothes I had at night and hung them by the furnace in the basement to dry. My good dress slacks came from Goodwill and were always pressed with the front pleat precise. The jeans that I wore to school and work were likewise clean and ironed, and I polished my shoes every night.

With the late hours of my job and the way I was dressing, my mother's naturally suspicious nature drew all the wrong conclusions. Her suspicions only heightened once I started keeping company with Mickey, Hazel's 21-year-old son.

One day Mickey had shown up at his mother's restaurant in Western clothes.

"Why are you dressed like that?" I asked, curious.

Mickey's answer was that he owned horses, and, one Saturday, I went along to the stables on the East side of Detroit to see for myself. Not only did Mickey own a white stallion, but he had a pinto that he let me ride, and when asked if he was willing to sell the horse to me, he said "yes." From then on, I was with Mickey at the stables every chance I got.

There were many reasons that my mother Grace distrusted males. She had experienced violence at the hands of her father growing up, her marriage to my father had failed, and, as Leon and I grew older, she especially worried about me getting in to bad company. Now, she grew increasingly suspicious as I hung around with Mickey, an older Black male, and saved money for a horse of all things! I wasn't acting like a typical Black teenager in Detroit—that was for sure.

"You're going to have the police around here!" she warned, for no reason that was apparent to me. I was doing nothing wrong. What was she talking about?

Meanwhile Mickey was taking me around, introducing me to other Black "horse people."

My boss, Hazel, thought that I was eighteen. I looked, dressed and acted like an older teenager—not the 15-year-old that I was—and, after a while, Hazel made me her night manager. I juggled my time even more between school and two jobs, trying to make it home from Hazel's by midnight to satisfy my mother's curfew. (In fact, there was an 11 p.m. curfew in Detroit streets, but the police never bothered me much.)

One Friday, Hazel caught her cook stealing and fired him on the spot. It put her in a pickle. She called me at Spitzer's and begged for some help, asking me to get to work at the Chicken Shack early.

"Have you ever made potato salad?" Hazel asked me.

The truthful answer was "no," I never had, but always ready for a challenge, I replied that "yes" I had made it.

Hazel told me to go ahead and make up the usual 100 portions of potato salad—the potatoes were all cut up, a gallon of mayonnaise and the other ingredients and condiments stood ready to go. I was to call Hazel when I had it put together, and have it approved. Instead, when I was finished, I tasted it. In my opinion, it didn't taste too good.

Something told me to try mustard. Two big dollops of mustard went in to the potato salad. Hmmm! It tasted much better.

"I'm finished," I called out.

"What in the hell have you done, boy?" screeched Hazel when she saw the yellow-tinged potato salad. But she tried it and then tried it again. "Looks like baby shit, boy, but it tastes pretty good!"

And that's how Hazel's Chicken Shack potato salad went from white to yellow.

Next came, "Have you ever made chili?"

I experimented with all kinds of spices until the chili came out the way I wanted it to taste. Then, within a week, the secret batter for the fried shrimp was entrusted to me with the warning, "If you tell anyone the recipe, I'll kill you!"

So, in a short span of time, the 15-year-old night manager at Hazel's Chicken Shack was preparing a good portion of Hazel's menu items that were famous in the neighborhood. I was also responsible for the inventory of food at the beginning of the night shift and making sure that the money and purchase of food matched. I regularly got out of work at midnight and a half hour later in the summer, working five days per week at Hazel's and six days a week at Spitzer's.

———◆———

By August, I bought the pinto from Mickey. I named him Amigo. There were never any riding lessons involved in my transition to horseman—I just got on the horse and got the feel of the animal, how it moved, and rode.

One day Mickey asked, "How would you like to ride in the State Fair Parade?" They wanted a Black kid to ride, and, as usual, I was game. I had the horse, now all I needed was the outfit. With the additional wages from Hazel's, I could swing it.

At Griswold's western store, downtown Detroit, I bought the whole shebang: black and white western boots, black western shirt with white piping, black hat, white silk neckerchief, and a cowhide belt. When I got home with my purchases, I got into my new Western duds.

"Boy. What are doing with all those cowboy clothes on?" my mother asked, incredulously.

"I'm going to be in the Michigan State Fair Parade," I replied, but Grace never believed me. Two of her sisters, Aunt Mattie and Fatso, who both liked me, were happy and congratulated me.

Picture this. I stroll out of the door onto 12th Street, down past the houses, to the local businesses, catching a glimpse of myself in shop windows. I look sharp! I casually go in to Cunningham's drug store and sit at the counter for a hot dog, then out the door and down towards Spitzer's.

"Hey, Cowboy!" someone calls.

"Hello, Tex!" another greets me.

I just smile in return. Inside, I am somewhat petrified. I didn't reckon on this amount of attention! But I must stay cool—after all, I am Lash Laroo and Wild Bill Elliot personified, with a dash of Hopalong Cassidy, Gene Autry, and Roy Rogers. I have the tradition of my Western heroes riding on my shoulders.

I stop in at Spitzer's, Hazel's, and Mr. Jack's, then the bakery where I get a brownie, and then go on home where Leon admires my black, western hat, and tries it on.

———— ✦ ————

On the day of the parade, Mickey gives me a ride, which is a blessing—otherwise I would be wrestling my saddle onto the bus (my usual means of transportation) while wearing my best western clothes.

It has been agreed that I shouldn't try to ride the full parade route on Amigo since we didn't know how well the horse will respond to all the loud sounds of the parade. So as planned, near the end of the route, I swing Amigo in beside the two celebrities with whom I am to ride into the arena for the big opening of the show: The Cisco Kid and Pancho. I am to the right of Pancho, who doesn't acknowledge the strange Black kid on a pinto who just joined him. The streets are crowded with folks waving and hollering. I wave back. I'm feeling good.

The three horsemen pause at the entrance to the arena, waiting for their cue, "The Cisco Kid and Pancho!" The music starts. The Cisco Kid and Pancho, draw their guns, reins at the ready and as they gallop into the arena—they fire. At the gunfire, Amigo spooks, rears up, spins to the right, and takes off at a full gallop, back the way we had come!

People scatter left and right. There's a woman with buggy, "Lady, get out of the way," I yell, holding on for dear life as Amigo dashes hell for leather to the safety of the stables.

There's a split door to the stall with the top half closed. Amigo careens straight under the upper door, as I fall off the back of the horse in a heap. I am decidedly shaken but not injured; my pride is hurt, but thankfully nothing else.

The lesson learned: movies are one thing; real life is another.

————◆————

As I began my junior year in High School, I was at an all-time low in hoping for a scholarship, or any success with education that would help me with a career. I was spinning my wheels, trying too hard and not being rewarded at an equal level with white students. There was no encouragement on my strong subjects, and no tutoring or mentoring available in my weaker subjects. Occasionally Eddie helped me with math, but he was seldom at home. In study hall, where help was supposedly available—everyone was told to be quiet and read. Most importantly the G.M. scholarship in engineering and design was not made available to me.

When it came to interaction with most students my age, I was uncomfortable. I still struggled with my stutter, and presenting in front of the class to rich, white kids, was agony. I couldn't befriend those kids either; I couldn't ask them into my home—I was ashamed of the way things were, and those other kids came from two-parent, stable homes, where the parents were involved in their children's lives.

Home life deteriorated even more. I was tired of the incessant girls' chattering and fussing, and, as I turned 16, my mother seemed to become even more suspicious of me and frustrating to live with. She constantly harped on me, "Where are you going? Who were you with?"

There was one friend beside Mickey, another older Black male, about the same age as my father, who took an interest in me. Amos was the boyfriend of Mattie Sue, daughter of Aunt Mattie, who lived in a big house near us. When Amos realized that I was an intelligent kid with abilities but frustrated with my circumstances, he showed me how to build things and work with wood.

Grace didn't trust this relationship either.

Things were coming to a boil. I was getting tired of working two jobs and then coming home to a chaotic house where I felt constantly under the magnifying glass of suspicion. I didn't want to return to the South, where I would have to sit at the back of the bus again, sit in the segregated section of theaters or only be served in Black seating areas of a café. I didn't want those constant reminders of my socially inferior status as a Black male. I was now used to the freedom of the North.

There was only one solution to the living conditions that were becoming unbearable. I called my father at Poole's in Birmingham and told him that I was going to join the military—would he please send up my birth certificate.

The military would take boys at 17 with their parents' permission, but I was going to try to get in at 16 by changing things—just a little. I tried to fudge the date of my birth on my birth certificate to indicate that I was eighteen. It didn't work too well. The recruiter took one look at the green birth certificate with the faded white spot under newly—typed black numbers, and handed it back, "Come back in a year, son," he said.

And so, I did just that—at the end of the following year, having obtained another birth certificate from my father, I approached my home room teacher Mr. Milland and told him, "I'm going to quit high school. I'm going into the military."

There was no reaction from Mr. Milland. I might as well have told him the sky was blue.

In my heart, I was hoping for someone at school to protest, for anyone to care enough to affirm that I had potential for college and was better than this decision. It did not happen. No one even asked me to give serious thought to my decision. I got the required paperwork signed, turned in my books, and walked out of high school for the last time, thinking, "They let me quit, just like that!"

As the heavy door with the long, lock bar clanged shut behind me, I panicked. I had last minute misgivings and tried to open the door from the outside. It was locked fast.

I turned and walked away with one thought running through my head, "Now I'm really on my own."

— 8 —

U.S. Marines: Boot Camp

The Navy recruiters were out to lunch when I arrived. However, the Marine Corps office was staffed, and after all, the recruiter told me, the U. S. Marine Corps is a department of the Navy. I signed up.

Later at home the telephone rang, "Is Albert Wilkerson there?"

Grace immediately thought it was the police. "Who is this?" she asked, suspiciously.

The recruiter explained that I had signed up for the U. S. Marines, but I needed my parents' permission since I was only seventeen. Only then did I explain to my mother and Eddie that I had quit high school and joined the Marines.

Oh No! Grace reacted immediately. She was not going to stand for that! She was adamant until Eddie stepped in and quieted her saying, "Let the boy do what he wants to do."

The following day my mother and Eddie rode the bus with me to Fort Wayne, and Grace signed the necessary papers. I took test after test and came out 83/100; high for the army—not so high for the Marines who were picky. I saw a doctor and was declared healthy. After the testing and medical exams were over, about 150 names were called alphabetically. Some boys were going to the army, some to the Navy, and about ten to the Marines. It was a long wait until "Wilkerson" was called, and I was in! The Marines wanted me. Later at the recruiting office, I was asked, "What would you like to do in the Marines?" Without having to think about it, I replied, "Work on airplanes."

Approval
Not Required.

SELECTIVE SERVICE SYSTEM

ORDER TO REPORT FOR INDUCTION

Local Board No. 37
Farley Building
20th St. 3rd Ave
Birmingham, Ala.

(LOCAL BOARD STAMP)

AUG 19 1958
....
(Date of mailing)

The President of the United States,

To .... -- Wilkerson V | 1 | 37 | 40 | 282
　　　　　(Middle name or initial)　　(Last name)　　　　(Selective Service Number)

.... .n Alley, North ....
(Number and street or R. F. D. route)

Birmingham, ... Alabama
(City, town, or village)　　(Zone)　　　　(County)　　　(State)

GREETING:

You are hereby ordered for induction into the Armed Forces of the United States, and to report

Southeastern Greyhound Bus Depot
at .... 624 North 19th Street, Birmingham, Ala. ....
　　(Place of reporting)

at ....7:00.... A. m., on the ....15th....... of .....September....., 19 58,
　(Hour of reporting)　　　　(Day)　　　　　　(Month)

for forwarding to an armed forces induction station.

Eugene Mungu
(Member or clerk of Local Board)

IMPORTANT NOTICE

If you have had previous military service, bring your service records with you. If you wear glasses, bring them with you. Bring proof of your relationship of the person you claim as a dependent if you intend to apply for dependency benefits.

This Local Board . furnish transportation to the induction station where you will be examined, and, if accepted for service, you will . be inducted into a branch of the Armed Forces. If you are not accepted, return transportation will be provided.

Persons reporting the induction station in some instances are found to have developed disqualifying defects since being examined and . be rejected for these or other reasons. It is well to keep this in mind in arranging your affairs, to prevent any undue . dship if you are rejected at the induction station. If you are employed, you should advise your employer of this notic . d of the possibility that you may not be accepted at the induction station. Your employer can then be prepared to rep.ce you if you are accepted, or to continue your employment if you are rejected.

Willful failure to report promptly at the place specified above and at the hour and on the day named in this Order is a violation of the Universal Military Training and Service Act, as amended, and subjects the violator to fine and imprisonment. You must keep this form and bring it with you when you report for induction. Bring with you sufficient clothing for 3 days.

If you are so far away from your own Local Board that reporting in compliance with this Order will be a serious hardship and you desire o report to a Local Board in the area in which you are now located, go immediately to that Local Board and make writte request for transfer of your delivery for induction, taking this Order with you.

SSS Form No. 252 (Revised ．　'．)　　(Supplies of previous printings shall be used until exhausted)　　U. S. GOVERNMENT PRINTING OFFICE : 1956 O - 390024

The three Black boys and seven white boys accepted by the Marines were told: go home, get your toothbrush, and be back tomorrow.

After lunch the next day at Fort Wayne, I boarded an American Airlines DC-10 and began the five-hour flight to San Diego. I was excited. It was my first time flying—and I didn't even have to sit at the rear of the plane!

The DC-10 swooped down over the rooftops and palm trees of San Diego just before daybreak. Upon landing, myself and the other recruits stepped off the plane into a cool, clear November morning. We were met on the tarmac by a corporal who rapped out, "Keep your mouths shut, eyes straight to the front."

The corporal took us over to a parking lot and loaded us onto the back of a truck. Sitting on the cold, metal floor was chilling. Few of us were warmly dressed. I was only wearing a T-shirt and jeans. It was supposed to be warm in Southern California! A short trip of two or three miles brought us to the Marine base and we were lined up outside the receiving barracks. It was 6 a.m. More recruits joined us, and then we were taken to the barber for haircuts. Translation: our hair was sheared off to the scalp.

Some of the white boys had been sporting natty D.A. (Duck's Ass) haircuts with their hair slicked back and styled. As their locks fell, the change in looks was startling. To me, some white boys looked comical with their pale, bald heads and protruding ears.

"Wipe that smile off your face!" came the order, when I was caught grinning at the spectacle of bald heads. "I said wipe!" I got the message, wiped a hand across my face, and adopted a safe, blank look.

As bald-headed recruits, we were herded to the mess hall in the brisk morning air, rushed in, and told we had five minutes to eat. Morning chow was ground beef with gravy on toast (S.O.S. or "shit on shingle") and eggs with a green tinge (powdered eggs that had sat too long).

The directive was, "Take as much as you want, but eat all you take." The method of requesting a menu item was to side-step down the chow line, facing the food servers, thrusting the metal food tray forward to the server with both hands when an item was wanted and pulling the tray back when not wanted. Unfortunately for me, I was so nervous that I advanced down the line with my tray permanently extended and ended up with a mountain of food. On command, I bolted the food down, threw up, and was ordered to eat that too!

After cleanup of our metal trays, we were back at the receiving barracks where we were instructed to get rid of all belongings. Some recruits had brought suitcases full of personal items. It didn't matter how much or how little, it had to either be thrown away or mailed home before we got our bucket issue—a galvanized steel bucket containing: a safety razor and blades, toothbrush and toothpaste, a can of Barbasol shaving cream, a small scrub brush and a bar of brown soap for washing clothes, two washcloths and two towels (white), a package of clothes pins (spring-loaded) a name-kit pad, a sewing kit (known as a housewife), and most importantly, a red Marine Corps Guidebook. The Guidebook contained a wealth of information about the Corps—the history of the Marine Corps, weaponry, rules of marching and formation, and the Uniform Code of Military Justice—all of which had to be learned in the thirteen weeks of boot camp. It was all vital to our life as recruits—even the bucket was utilized as a stool to sit on, and as a container for both picking up trash and washing windows and floors.

Early years in the Marine Corps.

Still in civilian clothes on our first day, we were put on a clean-up detail. We had not slept in a long time (few had slept on the plane), but we were kept busy as we waited for the 75 recruits needed to form a platoon.

"Who can run a buffer?" asked the drill instructor.

"I can," I answered, although I had only seen a buffer being used.

"I can, Sir!" was the instant correction.

I wielded the great beast of a buffer for hours with short breaks for dinner and supper. Finally, I was finished at 10 p.m., fell into my bunk, and closed my eyes. What seemed like minutes later, I sprang awake to the earth-shattering sound of a coke bottle clanged against the sides of a galvanized steel garbage can. We rocketed out of our bunks, stood at attention, and were marched off in our skivvies while our bunks were checked to see who had peed in the night.

Finally, that morning after mess hall, head call, and clean up, the magic number of 75 recruits was reached and Platoon 1002 was formed along with three other platoons. The new recruits were marched off to clothing. After body and feet measurements, utilities were issued: pants, shirts, underwear, socks and cover. My 9½ EE boots fit, but everything else was too big.

"Sir," I tried. "This doesn't fit."

"Move on!"

Recruits were issued a sea bag and the galvanized bucket went in first followed by utilities, two belts and a buckle. We marched back to the receiving barrack, changed out of our civvies, and threw them away or mailed them home. Mine were tossed, as I could not afford the postage. Then we put on our uniforms as instructed, and it was outside to form up for our first marching drill.

I had always thought I was tall, but I found myself two-thirds of the way to the rear of the formation with some really tall fellows from Texas out in front. One recruit by the name of Davis, blond hair, skinny and ugly, was up in front. He was about 6'6". His pant legs were too short, and his feet so big that the Marines had no boots to fit him. He wore black and white western boots for most of the thirteen weeks of boot camp while two pairs of custom boots were being made. He finally got them during the last week of boot camp.

"Shit Birds" the instructors called us, and the more seasoned recruits laughed at Platoon 1002 as we marched past to chow. We were all left feet, brand new uniforms and caps that didn't fit.

Housed in Quonset huts, Sgt. Tanner, a Black drill instructor (DI) had the recruits for the first three days. He began instruction. There was a wrong way, a right way and the Marine way for everything: marking clothing with a first initial and last name, folding and stowing clothes in the foot lockers, lacing up boots. We learned to do it all the Marine way. Everything was done at a rapid-fire pace. Sleep fast. Dress fast. Eat fast. Poop fast. By the third day, unaccustomed to the food and abbreviated time on the throne, recruits were getting constipated. Showers were Navy-style, two-minutes max. Step in, wet yourself, soap yourself, rinse off, and step out.

"Did you shave, Shit Bird? What did you shave with—a Hershey bar?" demanded the senior DI, who had joined Platoon 1002. I was seventeen. I had never shaved before. All I had was peach fuzz on my face, but I was ordered to shave immediately and did so—dry shaving while standing at attention, doing it by feel. The razor rasped over my dry skin and soon, blood trickled down my cheeks.

During the first week in boot camp, there was lots of testing. In Morse code, I was so nervous that I couldn't get my dots and dashes correct and got a low score. However, my average score after testing in Arithmetic, Reading, Science and Electronics, and Pattern Analysis was high enough to earn me a placement in aviation or electronics; a score under 110 earned a recruit placement in infantry, truck driving or cooking.

An M1, 30 caliber rifle weighing 9½ pounds was issued to all recruits during week one. We learned how to assemble, disassemble, and clean it. Your rifle was your girlfriend. Treat it with kindness and care. And DON'T call it a gun!

"Sir, I forgot my gun," an ill-fated recruit mumbled to the sergeant.

"You forgot your gun! Go in the hut. Take your utilities off. Bring back your bucket and your rifle."

Back he came, naked, except for his cover, carrying his rifle. His punishment: stand on the bucket with a piece of twine tied to his penis. One hand raised his rifle, and then the other pulled on the twine raising his penis. Over and over, "This is my rifle. This is my gun. This is for shooting. This is for fun."

No one could laugh or look at him. But every recruit could hear. One thing was certain; no one would ever call his rifle a gun. But there was a demeaning, twisted element to the punishment that I didn't like.

I thought to myself, "White people are strange!"

The exacting physical routine of boot camp went on through the first two weeks: running, push-ups, marching as a unit in close-order drill. And we got into the mundane routine of washing clothes by hand with a scrub brush, wash rack, and a bar of brown soap and hanging them up on a clothes line to dry.

The third week of boot camp brought a welcome change for me; I had mess hall duty. Recruits had to be in the Mess Hall by 4:30 a.m. and worked until 6 p.m. We weren't working for drill instructors but for cooks and mess men and that brought some relief. In the scullery, everything was metal and had to be kept spotless and shining. The behemoth of a dish washer was made of stainless steel and brass, and I was put in charge of it; I took pride in keeping it spotlessly clean.

Fourth week of boot camp, Platoon 1002 was loaded into cattle car conveyances pulled by tractors and taken to Camp Matthews in the hills above La Jolla. It was December 1955. We were to be at the rifle range for three weeks, living in pyramid-style tents with wooden floors, warmed by a small pot-bellied stove. To begin with, there was no firing, just familiarization with rifle positions and weaponry (22 caliber) and becoming accustomed to the firing positions for the M1. Later, we learned maintenance of targets, working with senior recruits, and pulling "butts."

As Camp Matthews got under way, recruit training for me was made much more difficult—miserable even—by the arrival of Sgt. Stingberry, our drill instructor. He was a lean, ramrod-stiff Marine, with a jutting chin, blonde hair and blue eyes. He carried a swagger stick topped with a cue ball which he used to reinforce his orders by whacking recruits. He picked on Mexicans and Blacks. Too often, I was kicked or hit on the head by his lethal stick, accompanied by, "Nigger," "Shit Bird," and "Sonofabitch."

For the first time, I wondered what I was doing here, being cursed every day and struck like some dumb animal that couldn't defend itself.

One morning Sgt. Stingberry went too far. Perhaps he had a hangover or just woke up feeling mean. He got the recruits out of their bunks at zero dark thirty. It was foggy and cold. We were formed up in our skivvies with our rifles and the sergeant marched us all over Camp Matthews. While we marched, we sang cadence. Loudly. And that cooked the sergeant's goose. An inquiry followed. Recruits were interviewed, including me, and Sgt. Stingberry was relieved of duty.

(By coincidence, not long after this incident, swagger sticks were banned in the U. S. Marines.)

The third week at Camp Matthews was qualification week. Recruits learned to fire the 30 caliber M1. At the 200-yard line, about two football fields in length, I fired my first shot and the recoil hit my cheek. Ouch! I adjusted my grip and fired again, hit the target, then fired again. Left-handed.

Many years previously, when I picked up a BB gun and fired, my father watched me, and then said in amazement, "Boy, you fired wrong-handed!" I had automatically fired the BB gun left-handed, just as I had done many things with my left hand from the time I was in Miss. Tigg's fourth grade class. I had broken my right arm and switched to using my left hand without difficulty. Now, using a rifle left-handed felt natural to me.

There was only one other left-handed shooter in Platoon 1002—the only other non-smoker, and we were placed at the outer edges of the extensive line of 75 recruits to provide for range of movement. This was not acceptable to the drill instructor.

"You will fire right-handed!" pronounced the sergeant.

I couldn't do it! For four days I practiced. And practiced. It just wouldn't come.

By Thursday towards the end of the day, he gave up. "You might as well shoot left-handed. You're not going to qualify."

That night I crept out of my tent. I told the guard that I was going to spend the night in the head. There I converted all the movements I had learned in handling the rifle, to shooting left-handed. By morning I was tired, cold and numb.

Reveille sounded, and the platoon went to breakfast and then to the rifle range. All seventy-five recruits in an extensive line, five feet between each recruit, with me and the other left-hander in the outer positions. 190 points were needed to qualify, firing from the 200, 300, and 500-yard lines. I lay prone. 10 minutes were allowed to fire 10 rounds, and I was the only person to take the full 10 minutes.

It was down to this. I needed a bull's eye to qualify. All the recruits were quiet—waiting. I fired. The target went down. Target up. Bull's eye!

There were no accolades from the sergeant, but I had done it. I qualified.

After Camp Matthews, the seven recruits who were Black were summoned to Headquarters. No one knew why. There, the case was made for us to become stewards. Three fellows who were the oldest, and who had prior service, took them up on it. Hey, said one of them—it's an easy job!

The three recruits, who turned down the steward job, were chewed out.

"You could work for generals," argued our sergeant.

"I didn't join the Marines to pick up someone's dirty clothes and shine his boots," I thought. "General or no general."

— 9 —

Twentynine Palms

After graduation from boot camp, I was off to Camp Pendleton for Infantry Training Regiment (ITR)—required training for all recruits. There, the young recruits of my platoon learned to fire machine guns, rocket launchers, mortars, grenades, and automatic rifles. We practiced climbing mountains and map reading and participated in simulated warfare and night firing.

One Saturday, I got a sense of liberty.

I had glimpsed the ocean on my way to Camp Matthews, but at Oceanside, adjacent to Camp Pendleton, I walked on a beach for the first time, smelled the sea, heard the waves break on shore, saw the big fishing boats out at sea, and strolled down Oceanside's long pier where people fished—making me think of my dad. I had seen the Great Lakes when I lived in Chicago but never the vast expanse of the glittering Pacific Ocean.

I was awestruck.

At Camp Pendleton the days passed with all the facets of training, drill, P.E. and the repetition that it takes to become a basic Marine.

Chow was important to the recruits; we burned through calories like a runaway freight train. In the mess hall at breakfast, there were always eggs, bacon, potatoes, toast and hot cereal as well as small boxes of cereal. The only brand of cereal was Post. One of the recruits in my platoon happened to be the grandson of Kellogg, from Battle Creek, Michigan. Recruit Kellogg told his family about the one-brand cereal deal and the following week a wide assortment of Kellogg cereals—Frosted Flakes,

Rice Krispies, Corn Flakes, and Raisin Bran—appeared like magic on the breakfast chow line.

At the end of ITR, I got my assignment. I was going for the first time (but not the last) to Twentynine Palms as an anti-aircraft crewman. But first, I had ten days leave, and I wanted to go to Alabama to see my father. I had no money, but I was told that I could fly free on military aircraft, and so I hitched a ride to March Air Force Base then boarded an aircraft flying to somewhere in Texas. From there I caught a hop on a Civil Air Patrol plane to Birmingham. It took me three days to make the trip.

When I landed in Birmingham, I called Poole's, and someone came and picked me up.

Of course, I was in uniform, and I was, no doubt, an unusual sight; virtually no Black uniformed men were seen on the streets of Birmingham. Moreover, although Black men had served in the armed forces during WWII and in Korea, few served in the U.S. Marines. When I corrected my father—who thought I was wearing an army uniform—telling him proudly that I was a United States Marine, he said, "Oh yes. I heard of them."

In the four days that I spent in Birmingham, my father took me around introducing me to his friends, and to Poole's to say hello to everyone. At night, I had to sleep at the house of one of my father's friends. My father was renting a room with no space for a grown son.

Before long, it was time to leave. My father bought me a train ticket to L.A. (The train was segregated until the Mason-Dixon line was crossed). When the train pulled in to Los Angeles, I was in a pickle. Twentynine Palms was a long way off and I had no means of getting there. Someone told me that I needed to go to the "Traveler's Aid" desk in the terminal and sign up. There, a kind, white female came to my rescue; she got me a bus ticket to Banning, then dug into her purse and handed me a $10 bill.

An ancient blue-and-white Chevy limousine pulled into Banning at 10 p.m. that evening. It was the stage line shuttle from Banning to the

Marine base and that night it ran through the dark mountains and pale sand of a desert that seemed endless. The old limousine was so packed with Marines inside and laden with heavy sea bags on its roof that it couldn't make it up one steep hill. We got out and pushed the old Chevy until it crested the hill—then got in—and the Chevy cruised on down.

Hours later, we arrived at the base in Twentynine Palms.

I reported to Receiving, was assigned to a barracks for the night and slept until reveille at 6:30 in the morning. When my feet touched the cold, concrete floor, I felt the grit of sand under my toes. Sand was everywhere. When I looked out of a window, I saw white sand and brown mountains. My eyes filled with tears.

"Where am I?" I thought dejectedly.

After taking a shower, dressing, and hitting the mess hall, I was taken over to the headquarters of D Battery where I reported in. Everyone who I met was white and from the South, including the first sergeant and commanding officer. They had the demeanor, looks and accent that had always spelled prejudice in my life. I felt nervous. My guard was up.

It didn't help when I saw where my bunk was. There were two squad bays in the barracks. The first was full. My bunk was in the second big, empty 100-bed squad bay. There was a rifle rack, two picnic-style tables, wall lockers and foot lockers for each empty bunk, bare windows and cold, concrete floor. Even this uninviting space was nothing compared to the hostile environment created by the white Marines in my unit; they were highly invested in making my life miserable. First, they short-sheeted my bunk and stood hidden in the darkest corners of the squad bay to see my reaction. When that didn't get the response they craved, they surrounded my bunk in the dark with blankets over their heads and flashlights shining up onto to white, distorted faces. Then, the "pranks" gradually escalated; the most potentially harmful was booby-trapping my bunk by disassembling it—then reassembling it held together by thread—which collapsed on me as soon as I laid down.

60

I was scared. I was only eighteen. My vigilance escalated and from that time on, I slept with a bayonet under my pillow.

One weekend, looking for something to do, I paged through the base directory for Special Services. Great! There were stables on base with horses for rent—didn't even cost very much—two dollars. After breakfast I set off on foot. It took me about 45 minutes to walk there. When I walked in to the stables, it was very quiet; just an old sergeant sitting behind his desk.

"What do *you* want?" he asked in a belligerent voice.

"I came to ride a horse."

"What for?"

"I just want to ride a horse."

Sgt. Mutton looked down at the papers in front of him on the desk—never looked up.

"Colored boys don't ride horses," he growled, dismissively.

I didn't know what to say. I just stood there.

Finally, he looked up. "You still here?"

Angry but knowing I couldn't argue with the sergeant, I turned and started walking the 45 minutes back to the barracks. My thoughts churned. I felt as though it was Birmingham, Alabama all over again. Why did everything come down to the color of my skin? "That sergeant doesn't know anything about me," I thought. "He doesn't know I rode in a parade with the Cisco Kid. Or that I stood on Blackie's back when I was only four. I can probably ride just as good or better than him."

Back at the barracks, I cleaned my rifle, washed clothes, walked to the PX, picked up my laundry, and bought a bottle of Pepsi. Then back to the empty barracks to wait for evening chow.

———◆———

I was in the lowest position in the unit, and my spirits were down. I pulled guard duty, cleaning duty, and policing duty. In addition, I had to rake the compound. Every day, I sat on a white-washed rock and watered down the sand around the barracks, then formed perfect rows of grooves with my rake. White guys ran over the sand, and I had to start all over again. It was the dumbest thing I had ever heard of—raking sand!

When I pulled guard duty, I walked around in my pith helmet, carrying a rifle, around the black shapes of massive equipment. Desert winds blew, tarps flapped, and bats swooped through the dark sky. It was haunting.

By day, I cleaned and raked…and raked.

Finally, there was some relief from the monotony. First, I was assigned thirty days of mess duty, and there were Black cooks who I could talk with. Then, I got some more freedom and was allowed to visit Los Angeles for the first time. A teenage Marine in uniform must have seemed like easy prey; a white woman, hustling drinks, called out to me—beckoning me into a dimly-lit bar. But I wasn't a lucrative customer. I only had twenty dollars on me.

Back at the base, I was assigned a cleaning detail in officers' quarters—making their beds and cleaning their toilets. Next, it was painting detail. Time was passing. The harassment at night was followed by the daily monotony of cleaning, steward duty and pointless raking. My existence at Twentynine Palms was becoming increasingly frustrating, and the closest I had been to my Military Occupational Specialty code (MOS) was guarding tanks in the middle of the night!

Each day, I passed the chapel, and one day I just walked in and asked to speak to the chaplain. I told the chaplain of the raking, cleaning, painting and the harassment—and how much it was getting me down. He just listened.

Soon after, a new Black kid showed up—Fred Smith; now there was someone I could talk to in the barracks. When Fred was put into the second squad bay with me, the pranks ceased. We were both assigned to mess hall duty for thirty days, and I got to know Fred better. He was a street-smart kid from Chicago.

Within a few weeks, Fred decided he would try to change his MOS. "Hey. I'm going to try out as a cook striker. Are you going to do it?" he asked me.

"No way," I thought. That was not what I wanted to do with my life. "No. I don't want to be a cook," I answered Fred.

———◆———

One day I was called in to the first sergeant. I was told, "You're being transferred to Alameda." And I was out of the desert in no time flat. I got my orders and a bus ticket, rode a Greyhound bus 500 long miles to Los Angeles, then changed for Oakland and NAS Alameda.

At the Naval Air Station, I was happy to see the faces of Blacks and Mexicans, many more than at Twentynine Palms—but my pleasure was short-lived. I reported in to the sergeant major, who looked at me, slammed his fist down on the table and yelled, "We haven't had any trouble with colored boys, and it better not start with you!" Why did the sergeant major do that? He scared the devil out of me!

I was issued my rifle and assigned my bunk in Section 2—a section of misfits: Mexicans, Blacks, goof-ball white guys, and old guys from WWII and Korea. However, it turned out to be a pretty good assignment. I was trained as Military Police and for the next two years my duties included guarding equipment on the big aircraft carriers docked at Alameda—the Ranger, Kitty Hawk, Midway, and Yorktown—to name a few. I stood brig detail and took part in ceremonial duties. I always tried to carry out each assignment to the best of my ability in hopes that my quality of work would lead to better things.

At Alameda, I worked hard to improve my speaking ability. The difficulty I had in getting out my first word—particularly when I used the tactical radio from the communications shack—plagued me. At times, I was mocked. Other times the typical response to my stutter was, "Spit it out Wilkerson!"

So, on my own, I practiced reading out loud. On night duty, I recited the General Orders aloud, beginning, "Take charge of this post and walk in a military manner..."

———◆———

Some of the Marines in charge were decent—others were not. A big, ugly white guy, Sgt. Crasco, couldn't find fault with me militarily, but changed my duty each time I signed up for a night class. I always wanted to fly a plane, so I signed up for Flight Simulator class. Taking this course would have helped me qualify for a ride in a jet, something I wanted badly. But, after I signed up, Sgt. Crasco changed my work schedule as usual. Attendance at this class, or any other elective course, was impossible.

One of the silver linings I found with getting my work schedule constantly changed was the opportunity to meet new people and make friends with Marines, naval personnel and civilians. I made friends with a Black family who lived in Berkley. They had a little boy called Daniel and sometimes I babysat on the weekends. When the Jones family heard of my love of cooking, they offered me the use of their kitchen. But there was a problem, the kitchen was a mess. There was no way I would ever eat or cook food produced there. So, one weekend I got hold of Ajax and steel wool and went to town on the stove, fridge, floor, woodwork and cabinets. Then, I cooked.

Next to the Marine barracks was the White Hat Club for low pay-grades and personnel under twenty-one. Everyone drank near-beer, or "green" beer which had a very low percentage of alcohol. It was hard to get drunk on this beverage, but I managed to do just that—getting sick on the beer and chili that I had consumed. I ended up with the "heaves" and "runs" at the same time and vowed that I was never going to do that again!

Blacks and Mexicans hung around together. It was the mid-1950's and there wasn't a lot of fraternization between whites and people of color, neither in the population at large nor in the Marines. I made friends with Charles—a Black, married Marine—and "Sputnik," a young Mexican Marine who bore this nickname due to his round, pie-shaped face. Typical of the times, Sputnik was picked on by white Marines.

Sometimes the harassment was not only verbal but led to vandalism.

Sgt. Gamboa who had fought in Korea owned a pink 1952 Ford convertible which was vandalized at night—the antenna broken, and a rock thrown through the windshield.

The targets of intolerance were not only people of color but also gays. A group of Marines went in to San Francisco on their off-duty weekends (every other weekend) and returned with a wealth of personal items: watches, jewelry, and money. They were going into bars, finding gay guys, and then mugging and robbing them.

One weekend they didn't return and were absent from roll call. They had been caught and arrested and were locked up in San Francisco city jail. Eventually they were released to the base and given a "special" court martial, reduced to private, fined and given a bad conduct discharge.

The drumming-out of the Corps was dramatic and final. The miscreants were marched four abreast in front of a lone drummer, the charges read aloud by the Officer of the Day, every button inscribed with USMC cut from their uniforms, and then they were marched through the base to the main gate and physically kicked out. It was a huge deterrent to any other would-be troublemakers.

———◆———

As time went on, my desire for a car grew. Buses worked to a degree—that's how I got over to the Jones' house in Berkley—but bus travel was time-consuming. I went in with Charles to buy a 1948 Cadillac with a V8 engine. The fuel at 25 cents a gallon was required for the engine, the equivalent of premium gas today. Payments on the car were $15 per month and the running costs were so much that the dual-owners could only afford to put in a ½ tank of gas one weekend and drive it the next. Within months, Charles reneged on the deal, and I gave the car back. I couldn't keep up the payments alone on my bi-monthly salary of thirty-four dollars.

In addition to transportation costs, a big-ticket item was the cost of keeping uniforms immaculate; summer khakis laundered and starched, or winter wool and dress blues dry-cleaned. There was also the necessity of an additional pair of shoes.

After some time at Alameda, I drew the attention of Gunnery Sgt. Braswell. He didn't appear to like me, but he did value my abilities.

"You work pretty good," he said. "Tomorrow, you come back and work for me."

For the next six months, I was taken off guard duty and instead did odd jobs for the gunny. I designed and built training aids, such as a proportionately accurate target that could be used at close range for simulated firing. I was given a free hand—essentially doing Braswell's job for him but in return earning some freedom, some status, and even the use of a vehicle. He realized that I knew a lot of people all over the base, so Sgt. Braswell assigned me a new '57 Chevy truck. To drive the truck, I needed to first get a civilian driving license, and then take the Navy driving test—both of which I passed. From 7 a.m. to 4:30 p.m. most days, I ran around in the gray, naval truck, finding parts, designing, and manufacturing training aids.

I still attended required classes on military subjects, such as the Code of Conduct under the Geneva Convention and Marine Corps History but, apart from those classes, I studied on my own. Through my efforts on the job and in my studies, I earned my first stripe. I was now Pfc. Wilkerson. (Private first class)

The extra freedom and the use of a naval vehicle had been observed by others, so when Braswell was transferred, and a new major came in, he took a close look at me. He saw a young, Black Marine, a lowly private, whose attitude he didn't particularly like. I seemed to be over-reaching in my desire to excel and to improve myself. From his perspective, I didn't know my place and was getting too big for my boots.

And that was the end of my relative freedom.

Under the new executive officer (XO), I was put on night duty at a large equipment supply facility known as the Annex. It was over four square miles, and my newly-assigned duty was to walk the area for four hours, carrying a riot shotgun. I wasn't used to night duty and got tired.

Sometime in the last hour I sat down, closed my eyes, and drifted off to sleep.

Before 4 a.m., the time I was to be relieved, the Officer of the Day came out to check on me. He couldn't find me. (Without radios, it was a visual check only)

Later the XO called me in. I was scared. What I had done was against Article 15 of the Uniform Code of Military Justice! However, no one but me really knew what had transpired. The executive officer tried to soft talk me: it would be "off the record" and I should "be a man and tell the truth."

"Yes, Sir!" I took the bait, told the truth, and quickly said goodbye to my stripe. I was placed on restriction for two weeks with extra duty, signing in on the hour from 5 a.m. to 10 p.m. with the knowledge that a minute late would earn me two added weeks of restriction. My period of good conduct since joining the Marines was at an end, but it would never happen again. It was a hard lesson learned and I felt that the XO had conned me. From that day on, I never got into any trouble.

One day, I was on duty at the main gate, when a taxi bearing a bearded man in civilian clothes came through. I asked for I.D.

"You don't recognize me?" asked the passenger in the taxi.

"No, Sir!" Then I recognized the voice. It was the commanding officer (CO) of the Marine detachment who had been on vacation in Brazil.

"Where's your stripe?" he asked me.

Later in the CO's office, I told my story and earned some sympathy from my superior officer who had taken a liking to me since becoming aware of my work with Brasswell. I got my stripe back on the first of the month, and my photograph was taken along with three or four other 18-year-olds who had been promoted.

All was well again. I got back the twelve dollars in my pay check that I had lost with my stripe, and, with my monetary status improved, I again wanted a car. This time I was helped out by a friendly Polish sergeant, who was known as Sgt. Ski. I asked him if he could find a good buy on a car, and Sgt. Ski came up with a pea-green, 1953 Dodge Ram in good condition and was so generous, that he co-signed for the car! I had just finished paying for it, when new orders came in for me.

— 10 —

Tank Commander

For the second time, I had orders to Twentynine Palms. This time I drove my own vehicle there—it was also the first time I had driven long-distance. I drew one month's advance pay and took off. During the trip, I was only allowed to drive about 750 miles daily because of safety concerns. There were no freeways to take me there, and the trip would take three days to complete. Caution was always part of the equation when Blacks traveled, even up North. I didn't risk motels; I slept in my car.

My new unit was the AAA Battery 3rd Battalion (anti-aircraft), and I checked in to my battalion a more confident and seasoned Marine than during my fledgling years. Because of my duties at Alameda, I had the advantage of being qualified for a wide range of weapons. I was, in fact, the only private first class qualified with rifle and pistol. In short order, I passed tests and got a promotion. On my record, I was stacking up as an exceptional Marine with only one screw-up to date.

The executive officer decided to make me a tank commander (TC) and, when he looked over my record, he shared a story:

"In Korea, when I was a pilot, a lieutenant, I did something stupid. The landing field was on a ridge. Down in the valley were South Koreans. I had the stupid idea to jack up the rear of the plane, line the sights up, and then fire several shots at the stilts of the hooches (houses). I was put on report and my squadron commander said, 'The closest you get to an aircraft will be firing at them from the ground.' That's how I ended up here."

Tank commander at age 19.

The captain was making me a tank commander at 19. Most TCs were corporals with sergeants in charge; none were Black.

"A lot of people are not going to like it!" said the captain. He continued, "When you first got here in 1956, why didn't you get any training?"

I told him about my prior unit's attitude and my subsequent transfer.

"Keep your nose clean and you'll go places," the captain advised.

Before I had a tank assigned to me, I had to train in the use of anti-aircraft guns including the calibration of aircraft speed, altitude, climbing, banking and descent of the target. After training, I was made tank commander of a Korean-era tank, an M42 Duster that was non-operational, with a crew of "green" Marines! The crew consisted of a gunner, driver, and two loaders under my direction. As TC, I had to

Marines stand at attention during an artillery inspection. Twentynine Palms.

know all jobs and functions of the crew. Most importantly, I had to get my tank functional—there was an inspection coming up in thirty days by the Inspecting General.

To get the tank up and running, I was back in the mode of aide to Sgt. Braswell; hustling, scrounging, and getting help from mechanics and radio techs. I used an auxiliary engine to power lights and to get the guns working. In addition, I polished the interior and painted it white and the exterior gray.

On inspection day, the crew stood at attention beside their tank.

"Why is this tank in maintenance?" asked the general.

I explained the situation: the main engine was still not running, but much had been accomplished. When the CO called the tank commanders in for a post-inspection critique, my crew got a "Satisfactory" for inspection and a good report.

In the months following, with the tank running on a repaired main engine, my crew (designated B-2) grew tight, hung out together and went places in my pea-green, '53 Dodge. We were all under 21 years of age. Having a car earned me some extra income. I made runs down to Mexicali on weekends, charging $5 each for the five Black Marines I carried. It was a 3½-hour trip one way. Like the other Marines, I enjoyed Mexicali—the food, the hospitality of the Mexican people, and the lovely, dark-haired Mexican girls. I even learned some Spanish.

This time around at Twentynine Palms there were more Black guys in my unit, including one guy from Oklahoma, one from Philly and two from Texas. One of the Texans was called Hank, and he could cut hair. He brought his clippers with him to the Palms, and he also used a straight razor, giving rise to his nickname: Straight Razor Hank. Hank cut the Black guys' hair in a style that was very short on top and razor-cut round the ears. The haircut drew so much attention that the general let it be known that if he saw another bald-headed son-of-a-bitch, he would throw him in the brig.

There were other rules established restricting Black Marines' conduct: Black Marines could not use any handshake that lasted over thirty seconds, and there couldn't be more than three of us congregating in any one space. That translated to us as, "Don't draw attention to yourselves."

In the meantime, the captain got the respect of his troops by arranging to have Straight Razor Hank cut his hair.

"I hear Hank can cut hair. Where does he do it?" he asked me.

"In the head, Sir! On a G.I. can."

The captain went in, sat on the can, and got his hair cut. This simple gesture helped keep morale high.

———◆———

One day, for a change of scenery, I asked permission to take my crew camping in Idyllwild. With permission granted, I went to supply for tents and camping equipment.

In the open air of Idyllwild, we set up camp. I was the cook (of course) and the crew pitched tents and collected firewood. We had a fine time, until Sunday morning just before noon; the nearby brush started moving alarmingly. We heard an unfamiliar sound, growling. It was coming nearer. A bear!

We broke camp, packed up hastily and got out of there in record time!

The captain asked about the trip.

"Tight crew," I commented.

Training continued. Bravo-2 shot at drones flying 200 mph and had one of the best records of hits. Then we got the news. In January 1959, the unit would be disbanded. Our tanks were obsolete, and jets were on their way in. But there were still assignments to be completed. The 1st Marine Infantry Division was coming to Twentynine Palms for desert warfare training, and the anti-aircraft tanks were to supply support for the ground troops—doing the job of combat tanks. Part of the training routine included M52 Dusters firing their pom-pom guns at objects on the ground either manually or automatically.

When the infantry troops arrived, there was more training on tactical support and my crew did a good job, excelling in accurate firing. I was awarded my next promotion to lance corporal.

———— ◆ ————

In February 1959, my unit went out to the desert for two weeks to practice what we had learned: desert map reading, land navigation, and recognizing landmarks using coordinates. We were also using live ammo. The area where we established base camp was in 100 square miles of desert.

Bravo-2 and Bravo-1 set off one day after breakfast under the direction of the platoon sergeant, Staff Sgt. Juarez. Before leaving, combat rations for lunch were drawn and water containers filled. I told Harold to fill up five water cans—a total of 5 gallons; each man in Bravo-2 would have a gallon of water.

Each tank held enough gasoline for a 100-mile round trip. As the tanks rolled along, stopping several times, I kept my eye on the remaining gas. The last time we stopped, I got down and went to the lead tank. Juarez was on top of the tank.

"Sergeant. I think we're lost," I said.

"What makes you think that?" asked Juarez, as he took a compass reading.

We got back in the tanks and took off. Soon the gasoline was at the half-way mark. We had gone 50 miles. It was past noontime, so we stopped and ate, but when one of my crew poured water out of one of their cans, he discovered that someone had polluted the water with sand. Out of 15 cans, only seven gallons were potable.

"OK," I said to my crew. "Take it easy on the water. We'll be back at base camp tonight."

We finished lunch and went back on our route another 25 miles, across miles of sand dunes and scrub brush. By then, I was certain that we didn't have enough gasoline to get back to camp. I pulled up next to our sergeant in the lead tank.

"I think we're lost," I repeated.

"We'll turn around," replied Juarez.

I pointed out that it was getting dark, it was also going to get very cold, and we had no warm clothes with us. Out of the 11 guys on patrol, only a few had snacks with them. There was no more food. And, most importantly, we were out of radar range. When we didn't return, search and rescue would be sent out. But meanwhile, we had to figure out what to do.

Juarez didn't come up with any ideas, so I took over. I found a dry river bed and positioned the tanks close to each other, then stretched a tarp from one to the other. As far as fuel, Bravo-1 had a ¼ tank of gasoline and Bravo-2 a little less; we needed this limited amount of fuel for the auxiliary engines. When darkness fell, it was freezing outside—the surface of the tank was icy. The crews stayed inside the tanks for warmth.

In the morning, we woke up and shared our snacks. There was no radio contact, and the desert landscape seemed endless. Nothing moved.

Two troopers took some water and set out to climb the nearest hill. They could see nothing. They returned hungry and dispirited hours later.

Since we had live ammunition, I suggested moving a tank onto a high, level surface and firing into the side of a mountain to signal our position, but Juarez nixed this idea. OK. How about we reconnoiter a designated perimeter for anything that could be used to help us? He agreed to this. A bandolier of rifle ammo was found. The ammunition was corroded, but the troops set about cleaning it and when it was polished up they loaded it into their M1's.

Everyone got 5 rounds and went out hunting jack rabbits, the only source of nutrition or hydration in the landscape.

I saw one rabbit, frozen in place, with its long ears erect. I aimed and squeezed the trigger, but the rabbit dropped its ears and hopped off.

The hunters bagged one jack rabbit, which amounted to one small piece of rabbit each. In addition, a soup was made from rabbit's blood and water, and we all sipped that. It was all we had of substance in two days. One trooper threw away a bone, and a verbal fight erupted.

That night the strategy for staying warm changed. It grew so cold that I suggested we dig into the river bank, lay down hot coals, then a layer of sand on top and crawl on top when the desirable temperature was reached. The troopers slid in to the narrow sand tunnels, hats and boots on.

On the third day, the order was given, "Don't fire unless you've got a shot." But not a single rabbit was spotted.

For four days and three nights, our troops were holed up in the desert. On the third night, while monitoring the radio, I heard faint bleeps. I tried repeatedly to tune in to various frequencies and to broadcast. Backwards. Forwards on the dial. Finally, I heard something, "Bravo-1. Bravo-2. Come in." Then the signal broke up. Again, "Bravo-1. Bravo-2. This is Twentynine Palms Search and Rescue. How do you read me?" The signal was weak and full of static.

Juarez was asleep. I woke him. We moved the tanks to a higher elevation and put the antennas up.

Another radio message came in, and then Search and Rescue lights were seen flashing three times—they were in range! Bravo-1 returned the three flashes. With that, the rescue unit was able to get our coordinates. Having ascertained the tanks' position, the unit had to return to base for gasoline, additional rescue personnel, and supplies.

It was two or three in the morning, in complete darkness, when the Search and Rescue convoy rolled in, bringing gasoline, corpsmen, soup and coffee. By 9 a.m., we were all back at the base camp. According to our gauges, we had traveled 100 miles in the desert.

After hot chow and a check over by the corpsmen, the captain called us in; first Juarez, and then the tank commanders one at a time.

The captain said, "Tell me what happened."

I recalled events, including the fact that Sgt. Juarez was trying to get our bearings by shooting azimuths with a magnetic compass standing on a tank.

"I figured you can't do that on a tank."

"Why didn't you tell him?"

"By the time I figured it out, we were lost!"

"Why didn't you fire the guns?" The only answer was that I had suggested it.

The captain turned the whole incident in to a training exercise, but Juarez lost a stripe.

———◆———

Within three months, the anti-aircraft unit was disbanded. I was sent to a 75mm aircraft battery and introduced to radar for the first time. Everything was changing. The new unit was also being phased out, and about two months later, it too was disbanded.

Because I was always trying to acquire new knowledge and try new things, I wanted to change my MOS. I requested orders to Lakehurst for parachute rigging school. (To pass the school, you had to jump using a parachute you had packed.) I got my orders and was on my way there via Brooklyn Navy Yard. While I waited there for orders, I went in to see New York City. The sheer size of the place scared me.

Back at the Navy Yard, while I slept, my orders came in. I wasn't going to Lakehurst. Instead, my orders read NAS San Juan, Puerto Rico.

— 11 —

Puerto Rico

The sea voyage from NAS Brooklyn to NAS San Juan, Puerto Rico took two days. My uniforms and all my possessions were packed into two sea-bags. To my dismay, only one made it through transit—the other was never found.

I was still somewhat disappointed that my orders to Lakehurst had been overturned but, as I checked into my new duty station and looked around, I saw that there were many people of color in San Juan, and that made me feel comfortable. I was assigned to a section of the military police; my duties would be similar to those at Alameda, and as I set about learning the routines of the base and the special orders that had to be enforced, I tried to keep in mind the high standards of my father. The life lesson that had really stuck with me was to be as good as I could be in all I did: standing duty on the main gate, going on patrol, guarding ships that required additional security, standing guard in the naval brig and throughout the days loving the spit and polish of my new assignment. My work schedule was one day on and the next day devoted to classes in military subjects, field exercises, and physical training.

A special work assignment was the disposal of WWII weapons and Japanese weapons via a boat manned by three Marines and two sailors. Orders were handed to me in a sealed envelope to be opened at a certain time on a prescribed course. The orders gave coordinates for dumping overboard the obsolete weapons.

On my time off, I began to explore and enjoy Puerto Rico: the people, the fresh fruit, the music, the sea air, the festivals, and the small horses ridden by gauchos in the back country. I fell in love with all of it. I prowled around Fort Buchanan and explored museums, usually on my own. I just didn't meet many Marines who liked to do the same kinds of things that I enjoyed.

And it was easy to get around. There were two different buses: an express bus that ran through town for 20 cents and the "nickel snatcher," a small, local bus, crowded with working class Puerto Ricans that cost a nickel a ride. On my travels, I got to know Puerto Rican people with whom I felt a rapport. It helped that I knew some Spanish from my trips to Mexico.

In time, I found fellow Marines who liked to swim and go spear fishing. I also joined the Marine Barracks Pistol Team that competed with other branches of the service, firing handguns: 45 caliber, 38 special revolvers, and 22 caliber semi-automatics. Our team did well in competition with the four branches of the service stationed in Puerto Rico.

———— ◆ ————

The music of Puerto Rico was everywhere: the jibaro, the bomba, and the beat of the steel drums. (In fact, steel drums were so much appreciated by the navy personnel that the Admiral of the base got permission for the Navy Band to be sent to Antigua and trained to manufacture and play the drums.) Often, I enjoyed Puerto Rican music in the company of Mac. Mac was a friendly, creative, and talented Marine buddy from Boston who played bongos and took me with him to local clubs where Mac sat in on sets with the band.

On base, there was always something happening at the outdoor theater and at the enlisted men's club, where there was tasty food and good music. Puerto Ricans were allowed on base every weekend. White guys had first dibs on Puerto Rican women.

One day when Mac and I had duty on the gate, a young woman came up to Mac and was introduced to me as his pretty girlfriend, Evadne. She was Crucian, and a base employee who lived on base.

Soon after, Mac said to me, "We're going out to the club. Evadne has a girlfriend—do you want to come with us?"

The friend was Winifred Maria Ferdinand, also Crucian, known as Maria, who worked for the wife of the admiral, commander of the Coast Guard base. One day prior to our prospective date, Maria walked up to the gate when I was on duty on her way to visit Evadne. It was clear by what I said to Maria that I already knew who she was. Surprised, she rolled her eyes at me. "Any more questions?" she asked.

On a Saturday night, the four of us went to a small club and listened while Mac played the drums. I sat with the women, not knowing quite what to do while they chatted in Spanish. Mac came off stage and danced with Evadne and then with Maria while I sat like a lump on a log. In those days, I had no beat, no rhythm and couldn't dance.

Despite feeling a little socially awkward, I started going out with Maria in the company of Mac and Evadne. Maria was attractive, shy, petite, and spoke English. Before long, she asked me over to the admiral's home; she was the family's housekeeper and had her own quarters. After serving the family dinner, Maria fed me spaghetti in the kitchen and began to talk about her life and how she came to San Juan. It turned out that she had met an Army fellow, got pregnant, and had a son. When that happened, her strict, Catholic family in St. Croix disowned her. Maria's mother took the boy away from her and since then Maria had been working in San Juan, sending money home to support him.

The Marine Corps Ball was approaching, an occasion that is of special importance to every Marine where the rich tradition of the Corps is celebrated in style on the Marine Corps birthday.

When I asked Maria to the Marine Corps Ball, I set in motion quite a lengthy process of getting permission for her to attend: the Admiral's wife consulted with her husband, who called the Marine barracks commander, who then called me in to discuss the matter. Only then was I granted permission to take Maria to the ball!

On the day of the ball, Maria looked lovely. The Admiral's wife had helped coordinate her ensemble including hair and flowers and satin shoes dyed to match her blue gown. After a couple of drinks, I was feeling pretty good and introduced Maria thusly to friends, "I'd like to introduce you to the future Mrs. Wilkerson."

To this day, I don't quite know what made me say it. I had just turned twenty, it was the 1950's, and my history of relationships with females had been complicated to say the least. I was attracted to women but also wary of them. The traumatic experiences of an absent mother in my formative years, an abusive stepmother, and girls chasing me in school, paired strangely with the pleasant experiences I had with senoritas in Mexicali—who I loved for their looks, vivacity, and sensuality. I had developed a special relationship with a lovely Mexican girl named Yolanda, but it was not sustainable across the miles. The good and bad of my experiences with females created a confusing mix of ideas about the opposite sex. To further confuse things, the Marine Corps message to troops back then was: we know you're going to go out there and have sex. Wear your rubbers. Stay healthy. Stay clean.

———— • ————

After the ball, I continued to date Maria. She was quiet but very nice and wanted to please me. We often talked in the admiral's kitchen as I helped with the dishes after the family had eaten. When we had time off together, I took Maria to different places on the island and although she never expressed a desire to go anywhere, she went along willingly enough. One day we went to watch a demonstration of Paso Fino horses where horsemen sat a glass of champagne on their flat-topped hats and rode the smooth-gaited horses without spilling a drop. The horse-lover in me was fascinated—Maria much less so. However, I brushed this difference aside as small in comparison to the gap in our ages.

"She's 13 years older than me," I confided to Mac.

"What's age?" was Mac's response.

Then one day, the phone rang, and Maria broke the news.

She was pregnant.

"Don't worry," was my quick response. But, in fact, I was worried to death. We had never discussed pregnancy. In fact, I had never discussed pregnancy with anyone. Not my parents, not my siblings, not my comrades.

In search of advice, I went to the chaplain, a Catholic priest. "What are you going to do?" the chaplain asked.

"I don't know," I replied, sick with anxiety.

"You'd better think this over," advised the chaplain.

Typical of the times and situation, the chaplain was suspicious about what kind of woman Maria was and contacted the admiral. Who knows what passed between them? When I next saw the chaplain, his words were, "You need to do the right thing." Those words echoed my father's advice on ethics and morals—advice I tried to live by.

———◆———

For Maria, I had a great deal of sympathy. She was single, Catholic, and in her thirties. She already had a child for whom the father gave no support. I was in a pickle, but if I felt distress for myself, I felt even more for Maria. What should I do?

There was really only one answer, "Want to get married?" I asked Maria.

"I guess so," she replied.

———◆———

I needed to get permission to marry from the colonel, and although I said nothing about pregnancy, it became clear from the colonel's words that he already knew. Those in charge had colluded, "If the situation was different, I wouldn't give you permission." But he did just that.

Maria was Catholic and, although I had attended Roman Catholic services ever since the nurse next door took me to her church as a child, I was never baptized. So, there was a lot of catching up for me to do in the Catholic faith: attending catechism classes for two hours every day for a month, being baptized, going to confession, and doing penance. The surfeit of new religious information added to my feeling of being overwhelmed. My life had changed dramatically.

Before the marriage, an officer in Puerto Rico called my mother, Grace. "Do you know your son is getting married to an older woman?"

My mother was not thrilled by the news, but she gave the needed permission for the marriage to go ahead. Subsequently, I called her before the wedding day. "That's nice," she said. "What kind of girl is she? Did you meet her in a bar?"

On February 26th, Maria and I were married by the priest, in the all-purpose base chapel in a Roman Catholic ceremony. Maria wore a white lace headscarf and a simple dress. Evadne stood beside Maria and a Marine friend from New York stood by me.

I was a corporal by this time and was promised a certain standard of housing due to my rank. But none was available for us as a newly married couple and, while we waited, Maria went home to St. Croix for a month. When she returned, we moved into a one-bedroom furnished duplex. It had a small front yard and a back yard filled with tropical vegetation, surrounded by hedges that were kept trimmed by machete-wielding Puerto Rican gardeners.

A friendly Navy chief and his family lived next door.

Maria was healthy throughout her pregnancy, and I set about the task of remaking myself into a "brownbagger"—a married man with a baby on the way. Money was tight, and, by necessity, I introduced Maria to commissary shopping. At the weekends, I barbequed fish, chicken and lamb in the small back yard, often with the Navy chief, who was becoming a good friend. As our friendship grew, I began to go scuba-diving with the chief and a civilian Frenchman every Saturday for fish and lobster, adding to our diet courtesy of the clear, abundant Puerto Rican waters.

And then Marcia was born. She was a pretty baby who I instantly adored. I had always loved babies, and now I had my own daughter. I delighted in sharing in her care—changing the baby and, when she could sit up, taking her out in a stroller. Her first bed was a clothes basket, then a dresser drawer and finally a crib.

There was never any word from Maria's family in St. Croix, until the sudden news that Maria's seven-year old son, Lester, was coming to stay.

Lester had never been away from St. Croix, but he wasn't doing well in school and needed some help. I tried my best to be that help. I

took Lester to the beach and did other things with him, but our relationship was difficult to get off the ground. One complicating factor was that it was not legal for me to have Lester stay with us in our quarters when he was not my legally adopted son—and his biological father would not agree to adoption. After some time, Lester left for relatives in New York.

Albert's stepson, Lester.

In 1961, a year after Marcia was born, I got orders yet again for Twentynine Palms to train on the Hawk Missile which was replacing all obsolete anti-aircraft missiles in the Marine Corps.

Our small family sailed from Puerto Rico into New York, picked up Lester who was going to try another round of staying with us, and then caught the Greyhound bus for Michigan to visit my mother, Grace, for a week.

Sometime during that week, I bought a black 1955 Oldsmobile.

On the day that we left in the Oldsmobile on our way to Alabama before heading to California, Leon hopped into the car to show me the way to the freeway. Once we made it to the freeway, Leon decided to come along for the ride to California too.

After we crossed the Mason-Dixon line, we didn't do much stopping. With both Leon and I driving, we only needed to stop one night and we all slept in the car at a rest stop—as always playing it safe.

In Birmingham, we visited with my father, stopped in at Poole's, visited Uncle Levi and then it was back on the road to California. Somewhere in Texas, the car broke down and we pulled into a service station—the car had the wrong voltage regulator installed and the part burned out. Thankfully, the service guy was helpful and went in to the next town for the part. We pressed on through New Mexico, along Route 66 into Arizona, and finally California.

Maria, Albert and Marcia in Twentynine Palms.

At the end of a long trip, I rolled in to the Amboy Hotel with my family on a warm, desert night, with sand blowing across the parking lot. Yep! It was Twentynine Palms yet again.

— 12 —

Cuba on the Horizon

When I checked in and began **work**, I was working with the Marine Corps' most up-to-date and lethal surface to air missile system—the Hawk missile. A new battalion was being formed, the 3rd Light Anti-Aircraft Missile Battalion (LAAMB), and I attended school every day for about six weeks. The CO of the battalion pushed hard. Sometimes we worked around the clock learning the system: radar, missile testing, electronics, and the launchers—each launcher having a crew of six to fire its three missiles. In addition, I qualified for an Explosive Driver's License which meant I could drive transportation trucks carrying explosives and missiles.

It was all new, intense and interesting. I enjoyed the new post—working in my MOS once more. The contrast between the lushness of Puerto Rico and St. Croix and Twentynine Palms was extreme. The difference between cultures was just as extreme particularly for Lester. He did not do well in the all-white school that he was enrolled in and was very conscious of his St. Croix accent. He became increasingly unhappy. Finally, Leon set off with Lester to take him back to relatives in New York.

As for Maria, it was a difficult transition for her in a new, strange desert town with a young toddler. Maria didn't drive and was shy with other women, however she didn't complain about the adjustment to a new place. She took care of Marcia, kept the house immaculately clean and never asked for anything. Living off-base meant that money was especially tight since the housing allowance just did not stretch far enough. Shopping at the commissary allowed us to buy larger, more economical pieces of meat and then cut them up to freeze. Maria made some Crucian dishes for our evening meals. When I found dry, salted fish at the commissary, she made a Puerto Rican version of Bacalao—a dish where the fish is first soaked to get the salt out and then cooked with olive oil, onions, and tomatoes and served over rice.

Food was a form of cultural sharing, and this brought us some new friends. I met a fellow Mexican-American Marine who had a little girl too. Our families had barbeques and made Mexican food together.

By the end of the first year, Maria, Marcia and I moved into base housing, which freed up some money, allowing me to buy our first television.

The intense training continued as the 3rd LAAMB worked to come up to the level of the 1st and 2nd Battalions. We worked around the clock on many occasions. Despite the grueling hours, morale was kept high under the direction of Lt. Col Ovington. Every week there was a 50-mile forced march that began at 4 a.m. in the morning. To offset the extreme physical fitness regime, once a week we all ate together, officers and enlisted. The meal was an early breakfast, and no cost was spared for the large spread we were served.

I was corporal of the guard, and guard duty included patrolling the buildings in the hot desert nights with warm wind blowing, keeping equipment free of sand. When sand storms struck, we had to button up the equipment and keep it free of debris. The command was on tropical hours and we began our day at 4:30 a.m., finishing at 11:30.

In the burning heat of Twentynine Palms, it could reach 130 degrees in the shade and keeping equipment cool was a daily chore. (I contributed to this endeavor by designing a container out of wood that kept fire extinguishers cool.)

———◆———

By 1963, the 3rd LAAMB was the newest but most proficient missile battalion in the Marine Corps, all three being stationed at Twentynine Palms. So, when the Cuban missile crisis struck, the 3rd

LAAMB was the air-defense battalion which would defend the country against the strength of Russian air power.

On a Saturday in October of 1963, there was a knock at the door. All leave was canceled, and the order given, "Report back to your unit."

Briefings followed briefings. All equipment was packed up ready for pulling out. No one knew where we were going, and it was labeled a drill. I was called in by the first sergeant. "Corporal Wilkerson. You are to report to the battalion commander."

"Can I ask why?"

"You are going to be the colonel's driver and bodyguard."

"Why me?"

"You are the only corporal who is a qualified driver and capable with a pistol in the entire battalion," answered the first sergeant.

When I was face-to-face with the serious-looking colonel, he stated, "You are my shadow and I will not be separated from my shadow. Anything you see or hear—you don't answer any questions. You are not to repeat what you hear."

This was unlike any drill in which I had participated!

During the six days that it took for everything to be in readiness, men remained on duty. With the help of a team of Judge Advocate General's Corps (JAG) officers, all Marines made out their wills. We were instructed not to watch television nor read newspapers. It was not until the last day before the departure of the battalion from the base, that dependents were briefed about what was happening. Married Marines were allowed home to say goodbye, but we still didn't know where we were going!

The first truck rolled out of the base at Twentynine Palms in the dark of early morning and the exodus continued all day, through one town after the other, stopping briefly to refuel and ending up at George Air Force Base in Victorville. As soon as trucks arrived there, they were loaded on to C-124 Globemaster II aircraft that were being used by Military Air Transport (MATS), through the big, front, clamshell doors. As soon as one was loaded with heavy trucks, missiles and tanks and a couple hundred troops, pilots were given the command to take off.

Once we were in the air, we were told that we were headed for a North Carolina base that was a staging area for the invasion of Cuba. However, the plane that I was flying in would never make it.

There were two explosions on the plane. Two carburetors had blown, and the second engine was on fire. The pilots shut that engine off and extinguished the fire, but the plane could not reach the East Coast. In the wee hours of the morning, we landed at a California Air Force base. This base didn't have the parts necessary for repair, and while spare parts were trucked in, all the heavy equipment had to be unloaded—about two hours of work—and reloaded onto another plane.

We took off, but misfortune struck yet again! This time the plane's heaters malfunctioned. It was freezing. The flight had to be aborted and the plane put down in Mississippi where the heavy equipment was unloaded and loaded onto yet a third plane. Finally, at 8 a.m. in the morning, the plane landed in North Carolina, on a base that was hidden by forest and only visible from the air, a staging area for the attack on Cuba.

Within two days, an advance party left for Guantanamo Bay, trained to set up portable communication equipment within one hour of landing and to knock out any aircraft threatening the mission, preparing the way for two assault units and the main body of Marines.

It was a tense time. President Kennedy had ordered the blockade that surrounded the island of Cuba—surveillance planes were flying over the island, battle Marines were on ships ready to launch a landing, and the Army 101st Airborne Division was in the air. Finally, the threat was downgraded. As for us, for two long days we waited on planes parked on the runway. We were in the ready position at high alert—ready for the command to take off for Cuba to face the Russian threat of a nuclear attack. Finally, Marines of the 3rd LAAMB were put on standby, moved from the planes into tents where we were to remain for two weeks.

———◆———

Thanksgiving was near. All married Marines were flown home for a week, and I was glad to get back to my family for a short respite, but all too soon the break was over, and I returned to North Carolina on a Marine Corps transport—a KC 130 Hercules, loaded to the gill with troops in full combat gear.

It seems as though the airplanes I traveled on during this entire time were prone to mishap!

In the pitch black of a stormy night, the plane was struck by lightning. There was a sickening jolt. The engines stopped. Then the KC 130 tilted sideways, dipping to the left, and fell! Down, down for about 10,000 feet! Most gear was latched down, but helmets were unattached and flew through the air. I remember looking into the eyes of my best friend, David Jones, sitting beside me. Only his face was now above me! Our unspoken words were, "Looks like this is it! We were going to Cuba to fight for our country—but we're going to die right here. Right now!"

After we made our peace with the inevitable, we heard a welcome rumble as the engines restarted! The plane leveled off and began to climb through the dark night and the driving rain.

———◆———

Upon our return to North Carolina, Marines were settled into quarters as quasi-calm returned to the political scene. Calm for the Marines on the base, however, was broken by a racial fight that erupted in the non-rated club between Black Marines primarily from the west coast and a group of white Marines from the east.

The cause of the fight was a common one: women. The majority of women coming to the club were white. Black Marines danced with them, much to the disgust of their white brothers-in-arms. MP's broke up the fight at the club, but back in the barracks, the fight erupted again. The crashing and yells brought me downstairs in my skivvies to witness the general melee and one short, Black Marine called Scott, built like a tank, throwing white Marines off left and right. I waded into the middle of things and helped break them apart.

Marines were sent to their quarters that night and then those in the brawl were put on restriction to calm things down.

———————◆———————

After the Russians agreed to remove their missiles from Cuba, things returned to normal. However, the decision was made to retain a Missile unit on the East Coast. Some Marines were given the choice of either remaining in the East or returning to California. I chose to return to Twentynine Palms and was reassigned to the 2nd LAAMB, while my friend David, was assigned to the 1st LAAMB.

— 13 —

Drill Instructor

One day in San Diego's main post office, about thirty years ago, I stopped by to pick up my mail. I was dressed in a smart business suit. Out of the blue, a man in his 40's, similarly dressed, came up to me and snapped to attention. "Sir!" he said. "You were my drill instructor. Sir!"

I was taken aback at this encounter. I did not remember the man out of the hundreds of recruits I had helped shape into U.S. Marines many years before. But such was the influence of drill instructors (DIs) on recruits.

———◆———

In March of 1964, I attended drill instructor school at Marine Corps Recruit Depot, San Diego. It was an eleven week, intense school that taught an elite group of men how to turn civilians into Marines. A high level of boot camp for seasoned Marines. A boot camp that included every task that recruits had to do—everything done "by the book." The book being the U.S. Navy Landing Party Manual (LMS) which we studied and followed to the letter.

At the end of each day, DI students studied for exams, practiced and rehearsed drills, prepared our uniforms, and kept up with hard physical training which included calisthenics and a tough obstacle course.

Perhaps, most importantly for me, this was the place where I came into my own. Drill instructors were taught how to teach. Inherent in the teaching practices that were modeled was the concept of teaching by example, and of being persuasive. In time, each instructor developed his own style within the guidelines—firm, aggressive, or even forceful.

By the time I attended DI school, I was a sergeant. I had graduated from NCO School, and had finally acquired confidence in my speaking ability. My stutter was still there on occasion, but I practiced and practiced overcoming it in the speech classes, which were part of the school.

It was a tough school. You had to study all the time—conscious that if you didn't pass the course it was a black mark against you and would stymie your career in the Marines. I worked hard and passed the weekly tests as well as the final exams in each subject. I graduated and was assigned to a battalion, company and section.

Drill instructor.

When DI school was over, I had two weeks to high-tail it back to Twentynine Palms, clear out of base housing and bring my family back to San Diego—a family that now consisted of Maria, Marcia and the newest addition, Mark, who was two years old. It took about four hours driving a 62' Chevy Nova for me to reach Twentynine Palms. There, I worked with Maria to ready the house for inspection and the sign off from base housing. Then it was back to San Diego.

In San Diego, there was a waiting list for housing. I did not want to rent. I wanted to take advantage of the GI Bill and purchase a house through the "rent to own" plan (in which monthly payments go to the purchase of the home), so I contacted a realtor and set up an appointment.

I found a house that I liked, but when I sat down with the realtor to sign the final contract, something was fishy! The realtor had switched contracts on me. The terms that I had first seen and agreed to had been changed, so I took the questionable contract and the original to the base legal officer who then wrote a letter to the shady realtor.

"Well, I'm sorry," said the realtor after I turned down a $275 incentive to close the deal. "You've gotta' start trusting someone someday."

A second realtor did not help much with that trust factor. I made the appointment by phone with a female realtor. When I turned up at her office, she was sitting at her desk: a small, white lady, wearing eyeglasses and an expressionless face. "Yes. Can I help you?"

"I've got an appointment," I replied, introducing myself.

"I'm sorry. We don't have an appointment for you on the books."

I knew what was going on. It didn't need an explanation. The Fair Housing Act had not yet been passed. Discrimination against Blacks in housing was common.

"Thank you very much," I said and walked out the door.

———◆———

As a junior drill instructor, I was assigned to a team of five, consisting of a platoon commander, the senior DI, and four other drill instructors in India Company, 3rd Battalion. The section that I joined was near graduation. After two subsequent platoons, I joined a senior drill instructor who was seven years my senior and a Korean War veteran. We formed one of the few Black DI teams in the battalion, and like all Black DI teams, we needed to be better than the best. We needed to be immaculate—hair, uniforms, drills, everything. To that end, the barbershop, laundry and dry cleaning were free and there was an extra clothing allowance that helped maintain the perfect image of the super-sharp DI.

To fill the 75-man platoon, it often took four weeks, and during that time recruits were picked up in the mornings for chow, marched over to medical and dental as needed. My senior DI and I were always working on marching: getting bodies to move in unison, forming recruits into squads, having them write numbers on hands or shoulders to learn order in ranks—tall guys in front to short guys in the rear, teaching them where their left foot was, looking ahead, not down, while marching, and moving like a machine.

Recruits came from all over the country, from diverse backgrounds and cultures, but they had to be molded into United States Marines. To that end, new recruits were taught everything: washing clothes, folding, stowing them, lacing up shoes, brushing their teeth, shaving, showering. Anytime they spoke, the first word was "Sir!" and the last word was "Sir!" Always, they had to listen to their DI, "Don't scratch. Don't fart. Just breathe."

Lying in their racks at night, at attention, I calmed them down from the hyper-alertness of their days. I reminded them to breathe and gave them a motivational speech, ending with the prayer, "God, Country, and the Corps."

Bedwetting was a serious issue. If one of the recruits had the misfortune to wet his bunk, he was sent to the bed wetter's hut, but first he had to clean, scrub and air his mattress. From that time on, he was restricted to drinking water only at mealtimes, and if the habit continued, he could be medically discharged.

All the training and attention to every detail added up to Platoon 359 being one of the best platoons that DI Washington and I trained. The average age was 18½. They were right out of high school. Westrate, Garcia, McWilliams, Flannery, Thrash. No fat boys, but physically fit would-be Marines who had no difficulty qualifying in the physical fitness test: 15 pull-ups, 60 push-ups, 200 sit-ups and a 3-mile run done in 18 minutes. The strongest guy was Sousa who scored 100% on the physical fitness test, and who went way past the required 15 pull-ups until he was told to stop.

At the completion of Phase 3 of boot camp, Platoon 359 was the Honor Platoon, proudly flying the top pennant and streamers, signifying their accomplishments earned during boot camp.

Being a drill instructor was exciting and invigorating; I adopted the persona, stayed in character and played my role. However, throughout my 3 years as a DI, I remained consistent in my desire to treat the young men who I was training in a humane way—unlike some drill instructors, particularly many white DIs that I observed, who were mean and even cruel. This type of instruction was counter-productive in my view, and led stressed, vulnerable recruits to self-destructive conduct.

One kid attempted suicide at the rifle range area by cutting his wrists. Blood was running down his left arm pooling on the ground as he stood in line for evening chow after being at the range. Fortunately, I saw the reflection of the blood and rushed the recruit to sick bay in time.

———— • ————

Training recruits was a tough assignment both on the Drill Instructor and on his family. Someone had to be with the recruits 24/7, and so with a team of two DIs—it was a one night on, one night off schedule. When a new platoon was picked up, the DI often did not go home for two weeks. It was very rough on home life.

In my family life, I was conscious of not being able to spend enough time with my young son Mark, and, from the time that Mark was four, it was clear that the relationship between us was suffering. Finally, when Mark was five, I knew that it was urgent. I had to make a direct effort to bridge the gap that seemed to be widening between us. I took time off to spend with Mark, taking him to various places including bases, and to restaurants, introducing him to folks and making much of him.

———— • ————

In my absence, trouble at the base began brewing.

I had trained Sgt. Bell to be a drill instructor, but Bell was made platoon commander before me. Something was out of whack.

I complained, and it got back to the company commander who

called me in. "Who do you think you are questioning my orders?" he demanded. The commander didn't like me and didn't like Washington. I was relieved of duty and sent to be mentally evaluated to determine if I was fit for duty.

Now in the Black community, psychiatrists were not to be trusted! You only saw them if you were crazy and that is exactly what I thought they were calling me, so I took the safest course of action and sat in front of the naval doctor erect and motionless, with eyes to the front. I was silent for four days.

On the fifth day, a Friday, the doctor cracked. "Sgt. Wilkerson, we've sat here for four days. You haven't said a word. I've done all the talking. But I want to tell you something."

I decided to respond. "What's that, Sir?"

"I'm on your side," said the doctor. "I'm not here to make you look bad. I don't see anything wrong with you." The doctor, it turned out, had checked on my records. "You're a very strong person," he continued. "As a matter of fact, I'd like to trade places with you and be a drill instructor. So, get out of here. Go to chow. I'll see you at 13:00."

"Aye, aye, Sir!" I said and did an about face.

———— • ————

When I returned at 13:00, the doctor was not there. There was only a Black corpsman in the office. "I shouldn't do this, but I'm going to show you something," said the corpsman, and let me read the commander's report. It read in part, "Strong will, intelligent; he has my highest respect; one of the best Marines that I have interviewed."

The situation improved immensely for me. I went home for the weekend, to report back to work on the following Monday. The company commander had been transferred out, and put in charge of the DI school. Then the week after the mental evaluation, Sgt. Major Brown called me in and told me that I had to report to Brig. Gen. Hackney's office at a given time, an order that required a fresh uniform and glassy-toed shoes.

When I got to the office, the sergeant major was already there with Hackney, and then a corporal entered carrying a folder. I stood at attention in front of the general's desk quaking inside. Something serious was in the works! Then the general began with the words, "To those that hear these present greetings…" Wait! To my ears, this didn't sound like I was being hauled over the carpet. In fact, I was being meritoriously promoted to staff sergeant. I was shocked!

"Breathe, Staff Sgt. Wilkerson," smiled Brig. Gen. Hackney. "Had you going for a minute there. Congratulations. You have one hour to have your chevrons changed."

I high-tailed it for the tailor's shop and said I needed a set of chevrons sewn on. And I needed it yesterday. However before the company commander sent me to see the psychiatrist he'd said, "You don't have enough campaign ribbons," and then set in motion the documentation that resulted in orders for me. And so, the period of calm that I enjoyed following the distress of the mental evaluation, was short-lived.

I was going to Vietnam.

— 14 —

Chu Lai

My initiation into jungle warfare and combat operations was conducted at Camp Pendleton, CA, in simulated jungle villages with bamboo huts. The indoctrination was for senior enlisted staff sergeant and up—some of whom had been retired, and then called back to active duty. By this time I was 25, one of the youngest going through the training

Marines heading for the Vietnam War were introduced to Viet Cong (VC) weaponry, and how to recognize signs of the enemy, such as fresh-cut bamboo, and trampled vegetation. They were taught how to traverse a rice paddy, to identify enemy weaponry like pongee sticks and the signs of potential "branch death" made from sharpened tree branches bent to their maximum that, when touched, spring back and impale the intruder. Hand-to-hand combat and "seven ways to kill a person with your hands" was part of the curriculum. Escape, evasion and survival training that included identifying particular vegetation and how to trap animals to eat were all covered. Snakes were identified including the most venomous—the Bamboo Viper. The most basic of Vietnamese phrases were included such as, "move fast" and "don't shoot!"

At the end of the month-long training, I was able to go home for a weekend and then ordered to report to El Toro, CA, for check-in.

From El Toro, the Marines flew 18 hours on a Golden Continental flight to Okinawa for five days of orientation at Camp Hansen. All uniforms other than jungle uniforms were turned in to storage. We were allowed very few personal items and no U.S. currency.

———◆———

In the early evening hours of November 1966, we left Okinawa in the dark and at 2:30 in the morning, entered Vietnam air space. All lights were extinguished. Window shades on the plane were down. The pilots were flying by instruments, landing on a dark runway only fifty miles south of the demilitarized zone (DMZ). In the plane's cabin, the Marines were quieter than church mice.

In the distance the flash and sound of loud explosions added to the tension of touching down in war-torn Vietnam. As we disembarked in to the pitch black of Da Nang, I could hardly walk down the plane's ramp; my knees were knocking so badly. No one knew exactly where we were. We had no weapons.

In groups, the Marines who had just landed were sent to various parts of the base, and then about 4:30 in the morning, we were put in to trucks and taken to a mess hall for a hot meal. After we ate, it was on to a distribution center, where on the walls, large chalk boards were covered with the names of units and locations: Chu Lai and Dang Hai Military bases, and more.

A corporal came in and read off groups of names. All 0369s in one group. Finally "Wilkerson" was called. My hand went up.

"You're going to Chu Lai, 2nd LAAMB Battery,"—located approximately 50 miles southwest of Da Nang on the China Sea. Only a handful of Marines were going there, and a few going to missiles. Marines had an hour to get their baggage collected; we would be issued weapons only when we got to our unit.

To reach Chu Lai, the transport airplane had to head out to sea and circle round to avoid enemy gunfire. We landed in Chu Lai at 10 a.m. and someone from Battalion HQ picked me up. I had to report to the sergeant major and then see Col. Black who I had known at Twentynine Palms.

Col. Black was glad to see me again and expressed his open-door policy if I ever encountered problems. "Wilkie, I don't want you volunteering for any combat missions—ground, air or sea. I don't want to hear that you are on a swift boat doing river patrols or on any gunships. Do you understand that?"

"Yes, Sir," I replied.

"We need all the staff NCOs we can get," the colonel concluded.

I was dismissed, and the sergeant major accompanied me to my unit.

Chu Lai was situated on a peninsula and my unit, MES39—first Marine Air Wing, was located on the sea wall overlooking cliffs that swept down to the beach. A MAG36 helicopter base and a MAG12 jet fighter base were on either side of the air defense unit. The 150-personnel unit was self-contained, and Marines defended their own perimeter 24 hours a day. Smack in the middle of the compound was the air-conditioned Battery Central Control (BCC) radar van.

It had been three years since I had worked in missiles, and I was a new staff sergeant and section chief. The unit called for three officers but was down to two, and I was promoted to platoon leader acting as second lieutenant and the unit's tactical control officer as well as the crypto officer, responsible for authenticating daily orders from Air Defense Command, and, in addition, responsible for two million dollars' worth of equipment. I worked 12 hours on, 12 hours off on the equipment, but my responsibilities to the troops and security was 24/7.

Soon after I arrived in Chu Lai, heavy rain began to fall and continued from November through December, raining for thirty-three days straight. Everything was soaked. I had never been so wet with no dry clothes left. On checking the perimeter, I discovered that the torrential rain had made the unit vulnerable to attack as it gouged out the ground, leaving gaps in the perimeter defenses. Barbed wire was strung, motion detectors and anti-personnel mines were planted properly.

The whole camp was swimming in mud, which was getting trekked in to tents and into the radar van. When the rain finally stopped, I initiated a common sense solution—construction of concrete walk-ways throughout the unit.

In 1966, Marines were armed with M14 rifles, but the service was converting to M16s, and I was sent to an in-country school to learn the new rifle and the M60 machine gun, and then returned to Chu Lai to instruct my unit in the operation and cleaning of the new weapons.

Working on the cement sidewalk in Chu Lai, 1967.

After my return, a new second lieutenant, Backman, arrived, a 6'5" Oregonian with big feet, who carried a double-headed axe at his side. I was assigned to train this new lieutenant, who knew nothing of the system, neither missiles nor radar. He became my personal headache.

The lieutenant was instructed, "Become Wilkie's shadow." That did not make him a happy camper. He did not want to listen. He did not want to take direction. Every time I turned around I seemed to fall over Backman's feet, as he breathed down my neck.

After a verbal confrontation with him, I went to the skipper, "I can't train this man!"

Backman was called in and the skipper chewed him out in front of me—an unusual occurrence.

"Listen to Wilkie! Do what he says!"

Things improved. In time Backman and I became friends and the big Oregonian even taught me how to throw his double-headed axe.

Upon my arrival at Chu Lai, I discovered a lax unit while at the same time many units were getting hit all over the northern section of South Vietnam. Standards were slipping; troops were getting sloppy. They weren't cutting their hair, weren't cleaning their weapons, and there was a lot of drinking.

In addition to the obvious danger from Viet Cong, there was a heightened danger for any officer, commissioned or non-commissioned, if they were Black. The services, after all, reflected the racial tension that was rampant in the United States of the sixties. Prior to my arrival in Vietnam, troops fired on a Black lieutenant while he was in his tent which he shared with a white officer. When I was promoted, some smart-ass kids, who resented my promotion, began saluting me, a seemingly innocent gesture, which in fact was dangerous. In combat situations, troops were not supposed to salute officers: it was deemed dangerous because enemy snipers would target them.

I had come from the strict regimen of recruit training to the laxness of the troops I found at Chu Lai. Resentment grew as I continued trying to instill order in the troops.

One morning I woke up and went outside. A rebel flag flew over a troop tent. When I went down to inspect the situation, I discovered that four Black and two Mexicans had been ejected from a twenty-man tent, making it all-white and predominantly Southern white. I gave the order, "Take down that flag! The only flag that will be raised in this camp will be an American flag."

The bad atmosphere intensified and deteriorated even further.

On an evening off, I went to the small staff and officer's club that had been constructed out of concrete, steel, and tin, overlooking the ocean—a place to try to relax for a few precious hours. I barely had time to sit down when a kid came to the door looking for me, saying, "I've got a problem I need to talk to you about."

It was dark outside, but the moon was out. Standing by the water trailer, the moonlight was in the face of the young trooper. What he was saying was making no sense to me, and I went on the alert. I saw a flicker—the reflection of moonlight on metal. The young Marine was sliding a bayonet out of his sleeve, trying to drop it into his hand!

"What's that?" I challenged him, and sprang back, drew my pistol, and hit the Marine on the left side of his head, knocking him down. "Damn. You just tried to kill me!"

"I'm sorry. Sorry. Sorry," stammered the kid.

Relieving him of the bayonet, I told the Marine, "I'll deal with you in the morning."

Up to this time in Chu Lai, only perimeter guards were armed, but after the Skipper heard of this latest incident, he ordered NCOs and officers to carry arms. I began sleeping with my 45 caliber pistol under my pillow and continued sleeping with one eye open, as I did the entire span of my duty in Vietnam.

One night, I heard canvas ripping on the side of my tent, near my head. I thought it was a VC but, as my hand slipped under my pillow for my pistol, I heard, "Are you sure this is where he sleeps?"

I recognized the voice, and I was out of my tent in a flash, catching one of them, still grasping a bayonet. I put my pistol to the kid's head. "If you make one move—you're dead."

Well, things could not have gotten much worse. Something had to change. I had got the relayed message that the Skipper thought I was overzealous—an implied criticism. I had to figure something out to change attitude, improve morale, and make the situation less dangerous for me!

———— ◆ ————

We ate poorly. The mess sergeant couldn't cook. On one occasion, I had augmented the disastrous daily diet. I commandeered a disassembled, unused pizza oven that had sat in a crate for weeks—got it assembled, gathered ingredients, and produced fresh baked pastries that the troops enjoyed. This time I upped the ante considerably. I decided to get all the corporals and sergeants together and do something that I knew I could do well—cook them a great Sunday meal.

The highlight of the meal was fish. I got two giant yellowtail from the local Vietnamese and cooked them on two field ranges that I set up by the club. In addition, I made fried rice from supplies on hand and served fresh fruit. The meal won over the hearts and full stomachs of twenty corporals and sergeants who left the meal much more favorably inclined towards me.

Great food had turned the tide!

— 15 —

Danger in Vietnam

In Vietnam, danger came on various fronts—even from children. One day, a small Vietnamese child slipped into camp to steal grenades; he got three but fortunately was caught before escaping. After this incident, things were tightened up at Chu Lai. There would be no more Vietnamese coming on base to give haircuts or to pick through trash—no more Vietnamese period.

Off base, at the Vietnamese market when I was buying yellowtail for the lunch that I prepared, I became aware of a small boy, about three years old, following me. It put me on the alert and so, when I felt my holster move as I was looking at the fish, I was ready. That small child was attempting to steal my gun! I slapped his hand, and the kid ran.

In the Vietnamese village near the base, children ran a food stand that advertised hamburgers. I stopped with some of my troops, looked around to check if it was safe, and then ordered a hamburger, which was served up on a French roll. But I couldn't bite through it, and it tasted "funny", not like any meat I had ever tasted. So, I handed it to a little boy who was watching me. The boy looked at the sandwich, opened it up, threw the meat away and ate the roll! One of the troops ordered an egg sandwich. Perhaps that would be safer. The yolk was very yellow. It was a duck-egg sandwich. Finally, I bought peanuts, ate some and doled out a handful to the group of watching kids. They, in turn, shelled them and began feeding them to me.

Food was one thing, but drink was another. It was too risky to try. We were aware that the Vietcong put ground glass into the ice.

Chu Lai Base, June 1967. Bay patrol.

Another danger appeared in the form of two VC frogmen in the waters adjacent to the base—one was killed and the second captured. In response, a swim team of four was formed with me as staff sergeant, the team leader. The primary objective was to keep the waters clear that lay between an island which lay 1½ miles from the peninsula and the base. We couldn't get hold of a Navy boat with which to patrol, and at first the team used a Navy life raft. However we definitely needed a more adequate craft.

Through the grapevine came news that upriver there was a sampan for sale (a flat-bottomed native, wooden boat with a sail and long sculling oar), and we made plans to buy the craft and sail it down river. We got up there OK, but it was a nerve-racking trip back, and our team stayed constantly on guard with rifles and grenades at the ready. (On top of the risk involved, this action had not been sanctioned by command.)

With the help of the sampan the swim team used scuba gear to check out the waters near the base. If the coast was clear, we took pleasure in our dives and shot some lobster for ourselves and for a general who regularly put in his request.

It became clear, however, that a barrier had to be constructed across the mouth of the bay between the peninsula and the island. Using the sampan, the team floated 50 gallon oil drums in situ, cut the tops off and filled them with rocks pulled from the sea-bed, stacking the drums three deep. I was working with two-hour air tanks, but with the extreme exertion needed for the task, they only lasted one hour. It took two days to build the barrier.

The use of the sampan was short-lived. One morning, we discovered the bottom of the boat had been slashed, presumably by the VC.

Additional "hats" that I wore were that of crypto officer and courier. When I was selected for the job of crypto officer I needed special clearance which was held up because Maria's father was a Crucian-born citizen under the Danish flag. Once I got all the necessary information from Maria my clearance came through. To serve as crypto officer, you needed to be an officer, and so I was made acting lieutenant. From my console, every morning, I checked in with Marine Air and the Air Force to ensure communications were clear and authenticate the orders of the day. The job of courier took me from Chu Lai to Da Nang and back once every two weeks.

One day I missed my flight back and hung out on some rocks that looked safe, a short distance from the helipad at Da Nang airport. I heard a C130 taxiing down the runway. Then there it was with its ramp down nearby. I ran up on to the ramp and called out to the pilot and co-pilot, "Where are you guys headed?"

"We're going to Chu Lai," the pilot called back.

"Can I come along?"

"If you don't mind riding a bomb!" the pilot replied.

The whole C130 was loaded with high explosives. The dangerous part would be taking off because of snipers.

"If we make it out over the sea, we'll be OK," was the consoling final comment before takeoff.

After circling out to sea and then heading inland, we landed safely on an airstrip, and I called for a pick up. The next morning, I learned that the helicopter pad on the Da Nang airbase had been obliterated, including the rocks on which I had been waiting!

One Sunday, some Marines and I were down near the water's edge, checking out the area, and planning to swim, when a group of nurses from the MASH unit appeared and introduced themselves. The nurses swam with the troops, and I showed one nurse how to use scuba gear. I introduced them to a safe place to swim, a sandy-bottom bay where no sharks had been seen.

Thinking I would perhaps see them later, I was making my way back through the base as it grew dark when I tripped over a tactical wire and crashed to my knees, tumbling down a hill. My left knee was injured and became swollen. I was taken over to the MASH unit, but when I arrived there I was asked, "Can you help?"

Marines from the 2/7 position had been overrun and were coming in wounded. I had to organize the walking wounded to make space in the tent for the incoming troops. Approaching one Marine who could walk, I told him, "Come on, Marine. Get up!"

"Leave me alone," the Marine snapped, loaded up his rifle and pointed it at me.

Finally, the incoming were taken care of, and it was my turn. I was X-rayed and, much to my irritation, medics stuck my leg in a cast from my ankle to my groin. I was going to be sent to the Philippines. Something I really did not want to happen!

"Skipper. I don't want to go. I'll stand all the watches in the BCC." The captain thought about it and said they would try it.

Thanks to the concrete sidewalks that I had laid, I was able to get around on crutches for six long, itchy weeks, relieved only by a wire coat hanger inserted between the cast and my leg, until I couldn't stand it anymore and chipped away at the cast and got free of it. Immediately, I began building up my atrophied leg.

———◆———

One evening the honeyed tones of Hanoi Hannah came over the radio and, as usual, everyone listened in to the good American music that was played during her broadcasts along with her derision of U.S. troops and predictions of which units would be hit. On that broadcast, she announced that the LAAMB units were on the list to be hit. Everyone was on alert—always on alert. Then in February, I got off duty and went to the club and, for the first time, did not stick to my self-imposed sobriety. I got involved in a stupid drinking game. Suddenly, loud explosions crashed nearby—mortars and rockets pounded into the base.

Then I was running hell for leather down the hill away from the staff club and 240-lb Jerry was thundering downhill beside me, when he tripped on a peg and rolled down hill. He was out cold. Too big. Too heavy. The only way I could get him to safety was to drag him by his feet, bumping his head over rough ground and tumbling him in to a bunker, then diving after him.

Throughout that extremely long night, I crouched in the bunker with Jerry and others as we waited for who knew what. We had our side arms but no radios—hence no information.

Jerry was blissfully ignorant of the previous night's excitement. "How did I get in here?" was all he asked the next morning.

Only one of the six missile units in this area of Vietnam sustained extensive damage requiring the others to scavenge for repair equipment and so, despite a big headache from the night before, I had to round up equipment on my base. This required backing a truck up a hill to access it. One driver had attempted it, but the road was narrow with a sheer drop to the ocean two feet from the right wheels. He couldn't do it. I told him to get out and took over the wheel. Up the steep hill for miles with my head turned, looking in to the mirror gave me a gigantic crick in the neck, and when I finally got up the hill and hooked up the truck to the radar equipment, I couldn't turn my head.

— 16 —

On Alert

By about half way through my tour of duty, I was exhausted. Standing long watches under high alert in a war zone and being constantly on alert for racist, personal attacks against me was wearing on my body and mind. So, when I had a chance to go to Da Nang to temporarily take over some of 1st LAAMB's duties, it was a welcome change.

While I was in Da Nang for the first time in this capacity, I didn't know that my Marine Corps friend David Jones was stationed there. When I learned, belatedly, that Jonesy was right there, I was eager to get together. Sadly, that was never going to happen.

On my next trip to Da Nang, I was told that David had been killed when his truck went off the side of a mountain. I was devastated. Jonesy, as everyone called him, had been my best friend. Someone I had enjoyed and cherished. We were also close in age and had done a lot together like playing football on the battalion team in Twentynine Palms. I had visited David and his family in Riverside with Maria and the kids. We had been drill instructors in the same company, at the same time.

I had a need to find the place that David died, went there, and took photographs of the scene. Many years later, I found David's name on the Vietnam War memorial in Washington D.C. and remembered him as my finger traced the familiar name, David Cleland Jones, etched in stone.

———◆———

Finding David Jones' name at the Vietnam War Memorial, 2000.

One night on watch, on top of Monkey Mountain—a hill that the construction battalion had flattened off—a huge blip was seen on the radar screen. It was a jet—but it wasn't U.S. I challenged the craft—"friend or foe?" The incoming was supposed to answer. (If the aircraft responded, "friend" they would then give their call sign which would be authenticated.) Nothing. I sent the signal four or five times. Still nothing! It was the early morning hours—not yet light, and I was the tactical control officer with two operators. They were locked on target. I called for an officer and quickly explained the situation. It might be a Russian bomber called "The Bear." The craft came on steadily, straight in. When we had a good lock on the aircraft, the "Fire" button lit up. I started the countdown, "5-4-3-2..."

Then the panel lit up, "Friend! Friend! Friend!"

My call of, "Cease fire! Cease fire!" averted catastrophe. Within moments a jet roared overhead, terribly close to the top of the mountain. It was a Japanese airliner that was lost.

———•———

The next morning there was excitement of a very different kind—involving the outhouse.

The routine for getting rid of excrement in Chu Lai was to first drain off the urine then siphon in gasoline and diesel fuel and set it alight. Wherever Americans were, black smoke billowed up every morning as poop was burned.

This particular outhouse was built on the side of a hill and excrement dropped about ten feet in to barrels. At the Chu Lai base, corpsmen had the unenviable duty of burning the "shitters," the rule being that they were not to be burned before 8 a.m. giving time for early morning relief. One new corpsman did not know the rule. In addition, he did not abide by the guidelines that said doors remain open while the fuel burned.

Unfortunately, the first sergeant was "taking a dump" as the excrement was ignited, and the accumulated gases blew up! Poop flew through the area in all directions. Luckily the 10 feet of separation between the sergeant's rear end and the explosion protected him, and he suffered no injury other than to his pride and, perhaps, his future peace of mind when relieving himself!

———•———

On night duty at Chu Lai, I was Officer of the Day on a 24-hour watch. Troops were in their foxholes in two-man teams with rifles, grenades and radios. The bunker at the apex of the unit above the sea wall was manned by four troops on anti-aircraft machine guns (quad-50s). During the night, I crouched, stopped and listened then advanced from one bunker to the next—giving the password when challenged then hearing the counter-password—round all five bunkers. It was very dark. I approached the biggest bunker. No challenge. Something was wrong. I went down on to my belly, sliding closer, then closer. I heard muffled sounds but could distinguish no words. Was it

VC in the bunker? Were the Marines all dead? My skin crawled with apprehension.

Slowly, I edged up to the bunker, a flashlight in one hand and my 45mm in the other. Then I smelled an odor like burning burlap. Pot! The troops were smoking pot. Inside the bunker were completely wasted troops, around them a scattering of white bread and outside a long trail of bread crumbs from the mess hall leading to the bunker. I made a radio call to the communications center to wake up the next relief and alerted the sergeant of the guard. Within 30-40 minutes the pot-smokers were abruptly hustled to the command post while the disgruntled relief took their places. Punishment was doled out to the pot smokers.

Next morning everyone was adversely affected by the incident: no toast for breakfast!

Another night when I was Officer of the Day came the ominous words, "We have detected something!" I went in to the communications shack. The electronic motion detectors had picked up movement by the sea wall! I told the captain and then quickly got over to the bunker nearest the sea. Damn! There were no grenades.

"Get down to the ammo bunker and get a case of grenades. Quick!" I ordered a trooper. The trooper was back in a flash with a case of grenades. I ripped off the top. Funny. The canisters were very light. I took out a canister and felt the bottom. "Clayton. You got illumination grenades!"

"Do I have to go back?"

"Yes! Get fragmentation grenades!"

The trip back for Clayton was not quite so fast, carrying a 25lb case of grenades and his rifle. When he made it back, I issued grenades all around. The object was getting closer, and I gave the command, "Lock and load."

One overly-nervous Marine fumbled desperately with his rifle. He couldn't get the magazine in. Then he started crying. "I can't get my rifle loaded!" I shined my light on him. The nervous Marine was trying to put his mag in upside down and backwards! I smacked one side of his face to square him up. But truth be told, we were all scared! We could hear it. I knew I couldn't let the intruder get any closer.

"Shield your eyes!" I ordered and popped a flare.

And there it was—a large dog! Dogs just didn't wander around the base or the village. So, first it needed to be established that it wasn't a ruse. But no one had broken through the perimeter, so the skipper was informed, "It was just a dog!" And the all clear was sounded.

———•———

On another night, the specter of danger was announced in much more dramatic fashion when rifle fire rang out from the right sector of the base. I climbed to the nearest high point then down on to my belly to peer over the edge, seeing what was going down. Troops were firing and receiving fire. I called for air support. Then as I watched the action unfold in the dim, evening light realized something was wrong! The incoming tracers of machine-gun fire were red not white. It was friendly fire! "Cease fire! Cease fire!"

From MAG 36, the Huey helicopters were coming in from the sea, rising overhead, with the unforgettable, Whump! Whump! Whump! of their blades. I signaled the helicopters that it was friendly fire, and they peeled off. Officers on the other side were alerted, and firing halted.

The story came down later. An army officer had got drunk and started firing his pistol. Troops of the 127th Signal Battalion thought it was VC and opened with machine-gun fire. After this near-disaster, army officers had to carry unloaded weapons unless on duty.

And so it went. Alerts. Scares. Perceived danger. Real danger. Troops who were doing their job, and those who were increasingly indulging in alcohol and drugs. Some troops were bringing back reefers soaked in various substances that upped the high of the marijuana, lowering their alertness and performance.

On the positive side, another Black staff sergeant, the same rank as me, came to Chu Lai. He was a little dude and a bit on the nerdy side, but I could talk to him. It made me feel less isolated.

———— ♦ ————

Off one day to get a shower in the officers' area, I noticed there was no hot water. I put on my thinking cap and came up with the idea of getting a pan of sand, dousing it with diesel and gasoline and lighting it under the oil drum that held water: it seemed like a brilliant idea, but it went awry as I tried to accomplish the task on the side of a hill. The burning pan tipped over, and the hillside scrub caught fire. In shorts and shower shoes, I beat at the flames with a shovel to the amusement of troops standing in line for the enlisted men's showers.

Yet another night. "Wilkie. Get up. We got a problem!" The MP's had brought in the sergeant in charge of communications. He had been caught after curfew cavorting with the local prostitutes. The gunny sergeant hadn't told the MPs initially that he'd taken a jeep, but one was missing, and he hadn't taken just any jeep but a Mark 83, an $83,000 jeep that housed all communication frequencies for the base. This was a major problem.

I knew that the jeep would be in the village somewhere, so I took a vehicle and scoured the area, checking all enclosed parking spots or spaces that might have been used to hide the stolen jeep. Coming up to a "hooch"

Grenade-carrying Sgt. Wilkie.

116

that backed up to a hillside with sliding glass doors on the front, I shone a light in to the interior. It was difficult to see inside. I wiped off the glass and tried again. There was the jeep—backed in between the bamboo poles that held up the roof.

I went in and started squeezing between the jeep and a pole to reach the passenger side of the vehicle. I carried a grenade in both breast pockets, as always, and, as I squeezed in, the grenade on my left snagged on the pole, while simultaneously there was a tremendous "Boom!" I froze. I'm a goner! My grenade has detonated! But no. I'm alive. The explosion is from the hill behind me. I felt my chest. My grenade was still in my left breast pocket, and when my ears stop ringing, and my legs no longer felt like jelly, I checked for booby traps, then checked the jeep to see if the radio frequencies had been changed putting the air command in jeopardy.

It was all OK.

With my heart pounding, I drove the Mark 83 back to the base and called the colonel. Subsequently, the sergeant was busted to corporal.

It had been a costly night of pleasure.

———— ◆ ————

In 1967, with approximately six months to go in Vietnam, I was trying to do my job to the best of my ability, trying to stay motivated, and trying to keep my troops motivated as well, but negative feelings about the validity of the Vietnam War were festering in my mind. The troops in Vietnam were aware of the anti-war movement that was building in the U.S. and then too, I had made my own observations. I had seen evidence of U.S. oil and rubber companies when I was on courier duty. I had seen young Vietnamese adults—obviously students—riding motor scooters with a stack of books strapped behind their seats on their way to school, and thought, "Why aren't they fighting? Why are we fighting for them?"

With four months to go, things got rough. New officers came in to Chu Lai, and they were green, fresh from the U.S. They didn't know what they were doing, didn't listen to senior NCOs, put troops in danger, and this all added up to them being gigantic assholes.

With the advent of the new officers, I was no longer acting lieutenant, but that didn't change my duties—I was still in charge of base defenses. The new captain thought there should be a machine gun nest in a bunker on the down slope to the sea. I led my troops in constructing one, as per orders. One major flaw in the captain's strategy was that when the tide came in, the bunker was washed away. Several times we rebuilt the bunker, the tide came in, and the bunker was swept away. Not only did the incoming tide present a major problem—the terrain did also. I was not going to rebuild yet again. I put it to the captain, "Captain! If I had a platoon down there, and we were hit, how would we get up? There is no way to get up. No way troops could assist us." Adding, "My mother didn't raise no fool!" I walked out on the captain.

The next day the office clerk told me to report. There was a fitness report for me to sign marked "unsatisfactory." After reading the captain's write-up of events, initially my reaction was, "I'm not signing this!" Finally, however, I signed it but wrote "signing under protest," and added, "The only way you can hurt me with this is to wrap it round a rock and throw it at me!" The captain was livid. He stood up, clenching his pipe between his teeth, strode out of the tent, failing to duck sufficiently under a guideline, his pipe struck the line, and he fell flat on his face. He got up, ears burning, and strode off.

The colonel sent the unsatisfactory report back to the captain. "I know Wilkie," the colonel said, (knowing that only two years previously I had been meritoriously promoted). "He's not that kind of person. This won't fly!"

The report was rewritten but was only a marginal progress report. For years it prevented me from being promoted, and it assuredly left a bad taste in my mouth. I continued to do my job, but I was coasting. Additionally, the bad feeling between officers and NCOs was affecting the troops, and the atmosphere was increasingly negative and hostile.

Then there were only two months to go until the end of my enlistment.

Finally, on a KC130 flight from Da Nang to Okinawa, I was able to say to myself, "I made it!" But with the troops on that homeward flight, I heard of one Marine after another whom I had known who didn't make it.

For two weeks in Okinawa, I was checked out medically, with the emphasis on my physical not mental health. I got my class A uniforms out of mothballs and then finally boarded a Golden Eagle flight by Continental for the eighteen-hour trip to El Toro, CA. No assistance was given to returning troops to get them from their landing point in the U.S. to their destination. I took a $50 cab ride to San Diego and arrived in the evening. I knocked on the door. Maria opened it.

I was home.

For twenty hours, I slept like a log. Then I jolted awake, scrambling for my service pistol as the sound of a siren ripped through my sleep. Battle stations! Maria was there crying, "Wake up! Wake up!" I grabbed her shoulder. Grabbed her wrist. Threw her over the bed and jumped on to the floor.

Then it was very quiet. All that could be seen of Maria were her feet sticking up. The sirens were those of a neighborhood fire engine. I was *not* under attack. I checked on Maria. She was OK. "What's wrong with you?" she asked.

All I could say was, "I thought I was being attacked."

———— • ————

It was not until I lived in Idaho, many years later, that I got any significant help from the Veterans Administration (VA) in neighboring Spokane, for the PTSD that plagued me from my time in Vietnam on. I still suffer from this condition that is one of war's curses. I cry out in the night. I dream I am being attacked. I startle easily, and

I'm hypervigilant. All this and more affects so many troops who have served their country. The VA hospitals are peopled by young and old, men and women who bear the visible and invisible scars of war.

Colored Folks Don't Eat Here

On thirty days of leave before reporting as a drill instructor at Marine Corps Recruit Depot (MCRD). I struggled to get back in to the pace of life in San Diego. I bought a 1968 Buick but had to learn to drive on a freeway all over again. Too many cars going too fast scared me into driving at 35 mph in a 65 mph zone. It was doubly important to get in some practice driving because I was about to set off for Alabama to pick up my father, who had been diagnosed with cancer. Doctors had given him three months to live. When I questioned Maria about bringing my father to our two-bedroom house in San Diego, she replied, "It's your Dad."

So, when my confidence in driving improved, I put the kids and Maria in the Buick and began the long drive to Alabama. We were on the southern route, and I knew what to expect in southern towns. The journey heading east, however, was uneventful. We had plenty of food with us and only pulled off in well-lighted places, mainly rest stops, when I needed a break.

I had called Poole's to ask about my father. Albert Senior was living in Poole's old funeral home which had been converted in to a rooming house, and I found my father—thinner and weak—in a room across from the former morgue where he had embalmed bodies.

We stayed for a week with my father's sister-in-law. There were no hotels for Blacks in Birmingham at the time. During that week, I talked to my father's doctor about taking the journey to California. Would it be more advisable to get a flight for my father or drive him home? It was decided that driving him to California was preferable, and Albert Senior, always positive about life, liked the choice. "I'm driving that Buick to California," was his comment to friends.

The Buick was loaded up with his few possessions, including his shotgun and a boat motor that was important to him, and he was installed in the back seat with Mark in the middle, and, under the kids' feet, a cooler full of food that would take us safely through Mississippi without the need of stopping to eat. We were on our way, heading west on Highway 10.

In Louisiana, we needed both gas and somewhere to eat—the cooler was depleted. We pulled off the highway into a small town. Where was there a safe place to eat? On one side of the street was the post office, with the Stars and Stripes flapping in the wind overhead and right across from it a Howard Johnson's. Surely that was safe. Pulling into the gravel parking lot, I backed in the Buick in front of the restaurant windows—just in case we needed a quick getaway. As I backed in, I had a quick glimpse of an over-stuffed white man in khakis dashing out of the restaurant and up to the driver's side. When I cut the engine and lowered my window, the white guy demanded, "What are you doing?"

"I'm parking my car."

"What for?"

"We're going in to the restaurant and have breakfast!" I retorted.

The silence from the others in the car was deafening. The khaki-clad man adopted the pose of the belligerent male: hands on hips, legs spread, brow lowered, and face turning red. He spat out, "Colored folks don't eat here!"

Slowly, I got out of the car, feeling the first flush of anger as my head swirled with images of the confederate flag raised over the camp at Chu Lai. I gestured at the flag flying over the town Post Office across the street.

"What do you think about the Vietnam War?"

"Not a damn thing!"

"What does the American flag mean to you?"

"I wouldn't know about that."

"Huh!" I said. "You're just wasting good air," and I opened the back door of the Buick and pulled out my father's shotgun.

"Junior!" my father's voice rang out in a way that stopped me in my tracks. It had the sound of his authority that made me snap to. "Get in the car and let's go!" I put the gun back and got back in the car, pulled out, turned left, then on to the highway, and kept on driving steadily for two and half hours until we were out of Louisiana.

We had now reached Eastern Texas. Everyone was hungry. I pulled off the highway in a small town and spotted a small restaurant with a Greek name. I pulled in, got out, and walked towards to the door. Looking through a window, I saw folks inside, but they paid no attention. The door was locked. I got back in the car and started to pull out when the door of the restaurant opened, and a man dashed out and came up to the driver's window.

He had an olive complexion, with dark, curly hair, and smiling, asked me, "Are you people looking for food?"

"Yes, we are."

"Well, we're not open until 11:30 but come on in and we'll see if we can find something for you." The man led us in through the kitchen, where whites and Mexicans were working, and then showed us in to a room with a window—the Buick sat right outside. He sent in a waitress.

"What would y'all like to eat?" she asked in a Texas drawl. We spoke up with a request for eggs and the usual breakfast fare, and then someone went out to a store with a list of what we wanted and hallelujah! Breakfast was served! On top of the owners' kindness in supplying breakfast, the waitress sat down and fed Mark as the family dug into their eggs, bacon, orange juice, coffee and cinnamon rolls.

When we were finished, I asked, "What do we owe you?"

"Not a penny!" was the answer, and along with the meal so graciously made for us hungry travelers, the owner gave souvenirs to the kids. It was the first hot meal our family had eaten in a day and a half. We could not have appreciated it more, and when we got home I made sure to write a heart-felt thank you letter.

But for now, it was back on the long road home.

Darkness fell as we drove into New Mexico, a state where Blacks could get accommodations. We secured two rooms and then went out to a KFC for chicken and drinks. The next day we were on the road just before the sun came up. It was a wintry morning with snow. The heater was on high, and we had a thermos of hot coffee with us.

I glanced down as I poured myself some coffee just as we came over a little rise in the road. When I looked up, we came over the rise and were way too close to a slow-moving car pulling a U-Haul trailer. I swerved to dodge the car and U-Haul trailer, skidded—trying to correct, and our car shot back over the highway, skidding again on the ice and finally flipping over on its side!

Maria and my father were scrunched on the passenger side of the car. They were shocked, but no one was screaming in pain. Quickly, I got out and then clambered up on the side of the car that was elevated and pulled the kids out. Maria and my father were still in the car squashed against the passenger side. Then the car teetered and started to tilt back.

"Run Mark!" I yelled, and Mark raced out of the way of the falling car as it righted itself. "Dad. You OK? Maria. You alright?" I called. Both said they were not injured, as I helped them out of the car.

The right rear tire had deflated, and the right side had caved in. It seemed as though we weren't going anywhere fast, but in record time a highway patrol appeared, and the officer called a wrecker. When it arrived, the operator changed the tire for a few bucks, and before long the Wilkerson family was back on the road.

From the time of the accident, it took us about twelve hours to get to California including a stop to eat and purchase food, and a rest stop in Arizona that boasted neither restrooms nor water, just a an overhead shade made of palm fronds.

———————◆———————

We had been home only three weeks when on the 27th of December, my father grew ill. I drove him to Paradise Valley hospital—a hospital with such a poor reputation that locals referred to it as "Death Valley Hospital," a nickname based on the reputation that so many people died there. We waited for hours in the lobby before my father was seen and admitted to the hospital.

Only three days later, at 3 a.m., I got the call that I had dreaded, yet anticipated, "Your father has expired."

I had been at the hospital with my dad the night before, watching over him as he lay semi-conscious, eyes closed, and as I watched him breathe, holding his hand, said, "Dad. If you can hear me, squeeze my finger."

And he did.

"What am I going to do now?" I wondered. With the death of my father, I had no Black friends to call for advice and didn't know of any Black funeral homes on the west side of the country. Having no alternative, I called Greenwood—a well-known cemetery in the white community. The spokesman said that they would pick up the body and "take care of it."

When I saw the funeral director, I could not help but express what I saw as irony, "My father was a mortician in a Black funeral home and now he's being taken care of by a white mortician." It was something that would not have happened in Birmingham, Alabama!

The initial arrangements were made. Greenwood said they would provide a small ceremony. Then, wanting to talk to someone familiar with my Dad, I called back to Poole's in Birmingham and spoke to the elder son, Ernest. "Maybe I'm responsible for Dad's death," I said, after describing the accident in New Mexico.

"No", said Ernest. "He was just hanging on, waiting for you to get home," then added, "I'll send you a casket—the best we have."

"Boy, your father must have been important to those people," said

Greenwood's funeral director, when the casket arrived. It was steel, waterproof and a $1,800 casket.

One thing was lacking in the planning of the funeral, a cemetery plot in which to inter my father. I didn't have the $150 needed. A family friend, Bob, came to the rescue and co-signed for the plot.

On a cool January day, Maria, the children, Bob and I were the only folks in attendance as my father was laid to rest (I could not find Leon and had not heard from him since I had shipped out to Vietnam). The short ceremony was conducted by a pastor from Encanto Baptist Church. I paid him his $25 stipend.

So it was, in this simple way, that my father, Albert Senior, was laid in his grave. After the short ceremony, we all quietly went home.

— 18 —

Reassignment

In January 1969, I reported to MCRD, Recruit Training Regiment (RTR). I was assigned to the Special Training Branch, a branch of the regiment that gave special training to recruits who had problems in the initial phase of recruit training, and/or were involved in medical rehabilitation. Recruits, who exhibited a lack of motivation, lacked discipline, were academically below the standards needed to successfully navigate recruit training, or recruits in medical rehabilitation and healing from broken limbs were among those sent to the RTR.

Starting out in the Motivation Platoon, I worked with groups of recruits who had been diagnosed as "passive-aggressive." Work with these recruits involved counseling and getting them motivated while still working on their training, including marching and physical conditioning. I was a good match for this platoon since I was not as aggressive in my style of training as many NCOs. I enjoyed this teaching experience, but I did not stay long in this platoon and was transferred after three months to the Medical Rehabilitation Platoon which had over 100 recruits—half of whom were on crutches!

Four weeks later, it was on to the Academic Proficiency Platoon. This was my best experience in RTR. The platoon was made up of kids who could neither read nor write—skills that were essential to get through recruit training. Many were draftees from Project 100,000 which affected all the Armed forces and drafted service men for two years. In other times, without the demands of war, these recruits would not have been deemed fit for the Marine Corps. Some of them had criminal records, and they all had low academic skills. The Academic Proficiency Platoon kept them for two to three weeks, and, with joint support from the Navy, tested them to see if they could be brought up to the standards needed for the infantry. I remember Joe from Michigan who only tested at the seventh month of first grade! Essentially, the platoon had six months to teach this recruit to read and write, or he would be released from the service.

———— ✦ ————

After some time in recruit training, I became aware of the discontent that was spreading through the Black drill instructors at MCRD. The number of Black officers was far less in comparison to the number of Black DIs on both the East and West coasts. In other words, Black DIs, who were responsible for training both recruits and officers for the Marine Corps, were not good enough to be commissioned. In time, an order came down to screen all Black DIs to see if they qualified to be interviewed for consideration in becoming officers. Five Black drill instructors in Special Training were eligible, and all were interviewed in April of 1968.

I was interviewed immediately following the tragic assassination of Dr. Martin Luther King, Jr. I stood in front of an Officer Review Board that was headed up by Captain Kulak, a short, aggressive officer, proud of his family history, proud of his participation in the infantry and dismissive of Air Wing Marines.

What had been my duties in Vietnam? What were the circumstances in which I had been made acting lieutenant? How had I motivated my troops? And then the questioning turned to current events.

What was the alias of James Earl Ray? The answer to that question was in that day's Los Angeles Times; the one paper that I had not read.

Kulak was immediately hostile. "You may have been a good platoon leader in Vietnam..." he began and then turned away, muttering audibly, "but you're just enlisted slime." And that was that. I was not encouraged to apply for officer training.

I was, however, promoted to platoon commander of the Academic Proficiency Platoon (APP). It was a position in which I flourished, and this really raised my interest in teaching. I devised ways to encourage the recruits to succeed, such as designing an Academic Proficiency Award for graduating recruits—a certificate that included the phrase, "Knowledge Is the Key to a Good Life." Each recruit who proved they could read the manual, and understand it, was presented with this award in a small graduation ceremony.

Unfortunately, I had to learn a hard life lesson about protecting material that I developed, when my second-in-command, a white NCO, stole the idea for the certificate and other documents that I had designed and slapped his name on them—helping him get promoted to lieutenant. I never again failed to claim material as my own.

———— ◆ ————

On the home front, I continued trying to do my best—trying to excel at being a father and husband. I volunteered at Encanto Elementary and was involved in my children's lives. The kids were small, but I firmly had in my mind that I should expose them to different things, and they were introduced to both horses and scouting at an early age. Marcia's personality was quite a bit more outgoing than Mark's, and she took to acting in a community children's theater group with enthusiasm.

When Mark was in kindergarten, it had became clear to me that I had not given him enough attention. I always thought I needed to spend more time with him to make him happier and to

Marcia and Mark, San Diego, CA.

129

shore up the military absences that riddled our early years together. After my Vietnam deployment, I took a month off work to take him on outings every day for four weeks. We went to the zoo, to museums and to the military bases. He took it all in and seemed to enjoy it, but it was hard to tell from his expression. On the weekends and after school on weekdays I made Mark my mission. I took him to bases dressed in a miniature military uniform and introduced him to many different folks. I snuck him in to my office. I had Mark watch the recruits. He quietly took it all in. On one occasion, Mark stood surrounded by a group of men all taking the time out of their duties to shake hands with him. Afterwards Mark's comment was, "Wow! That scared me Daddy!"

When Mark was 10 or 11, I took him along with me to work when I was a tank commander. It was against Marine Corps policy, but I got permission to bring him. I could never tell if he was excited or frightened—or just interested. He liked to collect things, so I gave him one or two casings from the tank shells that we fired the week he was with me, and he still has those, to this day.

Back at work after my month-long break, I realized that, for the first time in the Marines, I had the opportunity to take night classes. I really wanted to earn a high school diploma—a life achievement that had evaded me to this point. It had become evident to me that a lack of education in the Marine Corps was a hindrance, and although my GED equivalency certificate technically qualified me for advancement, I wanted to walk across a stage in cap and gown. I wanted to show my children how much I valued education, and I also needed to prove to myself that I could do this!

Enrolled in night school adult education, meeting at Lincoln High School, I found myself surprised, and somewhat put at ease, by the number of adults who showed up. Many of the students seeking a high school diploma were in the Navy. Once our classes were underway, I arranged a field trip for my classmates to MCRD to my regiment to view photocopies of famous, historical documents.

———•———

I had been warned before commencing duty in San Diego, that my chances at remaining there for a full two-year assignment were limited. With the Vietnam War still playing out and my MOS, my chances at being redeployed to Vietnam were high. So, it was not too much of a surprise when I got a message from my career monitor that I was to be sent for the second time to the war zone. It was an early warning of what was to come, but I did not intend to return to what I regarded as certain death. I would develop a plan of action and put it in place before I was due to reenlist.

And that is what I did. My action plan for steering my life toward upward personal growth and away from war was:

Earn high school diploma

Prepare financially to enter college.

Pay off my car.

Pay off all debts.

Establish a line of credit.

Save up a year of house payments.

First, I requested an extension in my present enlistment, which was granted. I then set about carrying out my plan, and upon earning my diploma marched in to the office and presented it for my record. The staff thought I was coming in to reenlist. That was the norm. No thought would be given to a Marine setting out on the course that I had determined for myself, and I had played my cards close to my chest. No one knew my plans.

— 19 —
Divorce

Close to leaving the Marine Corps, I would get up in the morning, do exercises with the kids, have them take military 3-min showers, get them dressed and ready for breakfast. I thought I had my two children a step or two ahead of other kids, because they woke up early and got their blood circulating and were strong and healthy with a positive routine. In fact, Marcia was the only girl in her class who could shimmy up a pole.

The only person who really brightened my day was Marcia. She would greet me at the door when I came home from work, hug me, and say, "Hi Daddy!" and "I love you, Daddy."

Marcia had been a delight in many ways. I had bought her a horse that she named Tonka. The first time she had been on a horse was a mechanical horse at 13 months old and even before I put in the dime to activate it she was making a clicking sound. I thought she was just a natural with horses, so when she was older I bought her one. Unfortunately, one day her horse began to race and then put on the brakes at a water trough. Marcia flew off the horse and landed on her shoulder on top of the concrete water trough. She never got on a horse again.

As for life with Maria...

Maria never learned to drive, so part of my responsibility was driving her to the commissary for food. One Saturday, attempting to have Maria be responsible for choosing food for the week, I sent her in to the commissary on her own. She was gone for a long time. Finally, she came out with two little boxes of food—not nearly sufficient for the week. It was difficult for her to make choices. In addition, Maria was uncomfortable with her accent. She was fine with Spanish-speaking people, and there were a few white couples with whom she felt at ease and one mixed couple, but, because of her discomfort, it was difficult for her to make friends.

On a very positive note, Maria consistently kept the house and the children clean—even to my high standard. One time a vacuum salesman came to the door and attempted to demonstrate the power of the vacuum cleaner he was selling, but when he vacuumed, the bag produced no residue of dirt due to Maria being such an excellent housekeeper.

But I was getting tired mentally in my marriage. I felt as though I had all the responsibility of the family on my shoulders. Most importantly, I felt alone with no sense of companionship. From childhood through adulthood, I had never experienced a fulfilling family life nor a nurturing relationship with a female, which had pushed me thus far to try to make my marriage work. Now, not knowing how to fix things, I started wishing I could exit the marriage. My greatest concern was how this would affect Mark and Marcia.

Not only was my time at the Marine Corps coming to an end, but I knew Maria and I were growing further apart. I was heading toward new frontiers in life, and she was not. I'd known for a long time that we were incompatible, in fact from the first day we were married—I knew that. But being young, I didn't know what I was doing and was mostly concerned about the baby she was bringing into the world. I was scared that if I didn't marry her I would fail as a father to our daughter.

After worrying and thinking about it incessantly, I came home one day and said, "I don't want to be married anymore." Maria was really upset, and I could understand why. But talking seemed impossible. I knew I would always take care of my kids; Mark and Marcia were 11 and 12 at the time.

I moved onto the base and went back and forth to visit the children. These visits didn't work out well, even after I included counseling in the mix. The military chaplain told me, "Take care of your family even if you have to go outside and get your loving." I didn't agree with his advice, and thought his counsel was very strange coming from a chaplain.

In about a year, I filed for divorce. Maria was angry, the kids were angry, and I was unhappy. However, after the divorce, Maria and I became better friends, and I stayed in touch with her. I was committed to supporting Maria and our children. Anything she wanted, I tried to accommodate. I gave her complete custody of the Marcia and Mark, paid child support and extras, and took the kids out. I saw that they finished middle school and high school. I wanted them in my life because I love children—and they were mine.

———— ◆ ————

After I left the Marine Corps, I was nervous about building a completely new life. I went into the Marines at 17 and left in my 30s. The Marine Corps was even more a part of my life than my marriage, so a career transition was a big step.

Right after the Marine Corps, I enrolled in college and, in addition, began working for the Department of Defense both during the day and as a police officer at night. I could study some during the day and take cat naps but then got only a couple hours of sleep at night. On the weekends, I worked at a department store and turned an overtime shift on weekends. Studying, working, studying, working, and taking care of my family constituted a busy life. I even tried Amway, trying to sell products to students and neighbors, but I didn't have a car at that time, so I couldn't deliver the orders and that didn't fly!

I got really burned out by this schedule which went on for 4 years.

One day, I heard that the San Diego Police Department had twenty seven Black officers walk off the job due to being denied pay raises—all but two Black officers quit. They were recruiting, and I went downtown to take all the tests.

The recruiter seemed tired of conducting so many interviews. "Well, I can either hire you or tell you to come back later."

Luckily he hired me. I went through the Academy and passed, beginning my new life as a police officer. I had to put my schooling on hold. I needed this job because my savings were depleted, and I had to earn funds for college tuition.

In addition to financial necessity, I wanted the job as a police officer because there were growing problems with police racially profiling Blacks and many people were starting to see cops as a negative presence. I naively thought that I could make a difference. But, once I started, I felt as though I had jumped from the burning fat of the military, into the fire of the police department.

When I was on the police force, I decided to continue my education. I had problems with this, because when my supervisor found out I was going to school, he changed my schedule, and I missed my classes. I became frustrated and cynical about the police department. But, being a rookie, I knew to keep my mouth shut. We had 1,100 officers, but only 20 were Black, and we were never scheduled on the same shifts.

One day, I walked into the Chief's office, gave him my badge and resigned. He asked what I was doing, and I replied that I was resigning.

"Why?"

I used the old standard, "For personal reasons," because I couldn't trust him or anyone else to discuss the discrimination and racism I had seen out on patrol and the racism I had witnessed at headquarters.

———◆———

I had a brief stint back in the Marine Corps as a recruiter dealing with civilians and talking with kids, meeting their families, speaking at schools and colleges. Working with people who were educated and had different lifestyles allowed me to see what I was missing out on in life.

However I had problems in relating to many folks; by nature, I was naïve, though not gullible. I also harbored a suspicion of certain kinds of people and was very afraid of old white men, and really didn't trust women. I was scared to open up to anyone, yet I was hungry for companionship. I had been in the military so long that everything had been decided for me and my life was very structured. While I was recruiting and interacting on a more casual basis with people, I became much surer of myself socially.

I was feeling so good about myself that when my commanding officer sent down a senseless order, I told him to stick it in his ear. He was so upset with me that he drove from Santa Ana to San Diego to chew me out.

"What do you have to say for yourself?" he demanded.

I asked him, "About what?"

The major started yelling.

"I don't have to take this," I said.

"What do you mean you don't have to take this?"

I said, "I don't listen to people who are yelling at me." He was furious as I walked away. Later, he was made to apologize to me by his superior officer.

I went back to my office after getting yelled at, and my spirits were down. I thought again, "I don't have to take this," and went to my lieutenant and asked to be discharged from active duty. I said, "I think I'm going to get myself in trouble. I don't think the way I did when I was a junior trooper."

He had to put it before the major, who said, "If he wants to resign, let him."

With few options, I went back the police department and asked to be reinstated. I was going back this time with a sense of empowerment and a feeling of standing up for myself. There was also a new chief who was supposed to be less biased. I was rehired, reassigned and reissued all the equipment.

So, I started my second round of being a police officer.

— 20 —

Being a Police Officer

I had joined the San Diego Police Department hoping, in part, that I could be a benefit to law enforcement and the Black community. After my time as a recruiter in the Marine Corps, I discovered for the second time that racism in the SDPD was common and it became increasingly evident to me as time went on.

I wanted to work in the Black community, but I always got paired up with a white partner when I was stationed in Southeast San Diego (where Black and poor people lived). There were two Blacks on my squad, Jake and myself. We asked our sergeant repeatedly if we could be partners, but we were always rejected.

"If we keep you in individual cars, the community will see more Black cops."

I didn't think that made sense, but I was always placed with a white officer until I was promoted and had my own beat and squad car. When I was with white officers, I was nervous and afraid to talk on the radio, self-conscious about them judging and scrutinizing anything I said. Despite this, I started building a positive reputation in the Southeast San Diego communities that I worked in, and that helped me overcome some of my fears and reservations.

———◆———

There is the spirit of the law and the letter of the law, and I applied a balance of both, depending on the severity of the crime—felonies, misdemeanors or infractions. When a felony had been committed, I had to arrest. Misdemeanors and infractions, I used my own discretion. But I was working with white officers who thought the only way to be a good cop was to make a stack of arrests. Our slogan on the side of the cars said, "Your safety is our business," and I felt as though some of the officers didn't uphold that. A fraction of officers were all blonde and called themselves The German Corps. They would harass Black civilians and even Black officers, and their conduct was an example of the most racist police officers.

The first Black sergeant was promoted in 1938 and the second didn't achieve that rank until in 1968. By that time, women had started to come on to the police force as well.

When I became a senior officer, my supervisor would put rookies with me to train them, but he would always place someone that they were about to kick off the force (always women and Black officers who had not made their probation). I saved quite a few jobs by helping these individuals shore up their skills. One Black female, didn't make her probation because all the male cops were against her. She had a nervous breakdown and was under medical care for an entire year; her hair fell out and she gained weight. When she won her case and they brought her back, she was put with me. I was told to watch everything she did and write down everything she "screwed up on."

Our first day out together, it rained in San Diego. We got a burglary call to a location where it was very muddy. The crooks we were chasing ran down through a basement, and I told her to follow their footprints.

She said, "I have to walk in the mud?"

And I said, "Yes, you do." I told her what the other officers had told me to do with her, and I wanted to give her a fair chance.

She said, "Wow, you're the first one with a badge who has been nice to me." I had her for two weeks.

During lunch one day I said, "I'm sorry I can't pay for your lunch,"

"Officer Wilkerson," she said. "We are not on a date," and I laughed. It felt good to help her get back on her feet.

The next officer they gave me was **Ben**. Ben had been on several trainings with officers. They were about to fire him. A certain white sergeant would take anyone who they planned to fire and would make sure that he failed his review. Ben came to me for help, and my supervisor agreed to assign him to me. I saved his job and even had him as a partner afterward. He was the only Black partner I was paired with during my time with the San Diego Police Department.

The next rookie I was assigned was Johnny who had problems because he couldn't do reports. Over many days of training, I showed him how to write his reports and do all his documentation. His speech was fine, but he was poor at writing, and I straightened him out. In all, I retrained five women and three men.

I was only ever given one white officer to retrain. Once when we were on patrol, we stopped a taxi that was tailgating. The taxi driver fought it, and we went to court. I remember in court the taxi cab driver gesturing towards me and saying to my white trainee, "Boy, you give these guys a badge and they think they own the world."

Then in court, referring to my trainee, the cab driver declared, "The person standing up there did not write the ticket and did not see the infraction." The judge then gave the cab driver a copy of the ticket and asked him to read it out loud and when he read, "Officer Wilkerson," the judge said to me, "Can you tell the court your name?" When I did, the taxi driver turned a dozen shades of red when he realized I was the lead officer.

While on the force, I delivered two babies. One I remember well. It was at the Greyhound bus station. My unit was 11H (H meant you were a single officer). In February 1975, "11H OB, Greyhound Bus Station" came on the radio. I said, "OB?"

And the dispatcher said, "Yes, OB as in baby."

It was a dismal, gray night as I got there and ran in with my gurney. The bus station restroom was full of bag women, dressed in raggedy, somewhat smelly clothes. They were all gathered around this young female sitting on the toilet. She was only 15 years old, illegally in the country, and about to give birth. There in the stall, with all the women breathing down my neck, the baby's head was coming out, and I could barely see between her legs in the cramped, gloomy toilet stall. As the baby slipped out I couldn't hold on to her and accidentally dropped her into the toilet!

I fished her out quickly, cleaned off the urine and toilet paper, put the baby in her mother's arms, and lifted them onto the gurney and then in to the station wagon that was used as an ambulance in those days, and then got them at top speed to the hospital. The baby was healthy, and the doctor said I did an excellent job. Relieved that everyone was OK, I was able to breathe again. The young mother named the baby Graciella. I'll never forget that name. She was grateful that I helped her, but that was the last I heard of her.

The second baby I delivered was born in the back of the ambulance station wagon as we drove her to the hospital. Mother and baby were both fine, with no medical problems.

Other than saving Black and female police officers' jobs and delivering babies, I also busted a lot of drug users for marijuana, heroin, crack cocaine, and other substances and over time was assigned to different squads.

On a call to apprehend a felony wife beater, I entered the house of the suspect. The dispatcher said he had a gun, but I still went in as he was a threat to his wife's life. It was totally dark as I crept toward an open staircase. I could see the attic was open and, in the moonlight, I could tell the suspect was standing up there. I quietly stood on a table to see if I could grab one of his legs and pull him down, but he started throwing boards down. Another officer walked in and unfortunately shone his flashlight on me so the perpetrator saw me clearly and threw a board right at me, striking me in my right kneecap, which began pounding with severe pain and swelling up.

To this day, I still have problems with my knee from that injury. I had to go to the hospital to get my leg in a cast, and I was stationed on light duty for several weeks. After physical therapy, the police department put me in the juvenile division, and I did intake calls. A friend of mine, Elton, was on the school task force, and he looked out for me during my stint in juvenile intake.

One juvenile case I handled was unforgettable. The girl was white and named Lisa. She was 12 but looked 22. Her father called the

police department and wanted her arrested because she was going through an identity crisis. She wanted to be Black, and her father didn't approve of how she dressed or her choice of Black friends. I talked to her mother then talked to her father. Because she was identifying with Black people, he completely rejected her as his daughter. My lieutenant said to let the case go and ignore it.

About two months later, we got a call from Oceanside. They had found a girl passed out in a

Albert and his friend, Elton.

motel. It was Lisa. Since she was banned from going home, she had gone into prostitution, had passed out on this occasion in a hotel and been sexually assaulted. Her mother called to speak to me, desperate for help. Since Oceanside was in a different jurisdiction, I could do nothing. I felt bad and told her mom I would help in any way I could other than officially, but I never heard anything further from them.

———— ◆ ————

At one point, I was so distraught about the internal racism and discrimination within the police department that I even thought of taking my life. I was in the department all night by myself, and things were not going the way I had expected them to go with my family life, nor with my job at the police department. I felt at the end of my rope, too tired to carry on. I had a gun. It would have been easy. I was sitting on the cold floor with my service revolver next to me, and I had put a bullet in the chamber, when my brother, Leon, who had come to San Diego, stopped by unexpectedly.

He said, "What's your gun doing on the floor?"

I told him, and he looked at me and said, "If you commit suicide, I'll kill you!"

I laughed because there was a lot of humor in that—even though for me at the time it was deadly serious!

———— ◆ ————

Near where I was living at this time, there was an upscale apartment complex that had some white residents who didn't like Black people. One night a white guy came to my door and put his finger in my face, "Nigger Boy, if you park that close to my car again, you'll be sorry!" I didn't know who this big, white fellow with the red, screwed—up face was.

I reached back to get my service revolver and said, "You better get out of my face, dude."

The next time he came knocking on my door he began kicking it. I grabbed my shotgun but paused long enough to call the police department saying, "There's going be a 187 if you don't get down here." A 187 was a homicide.

Officers arrived and took my gun, and I went in to the chief of police who was from Mississippi, to explain the situation. He played back the tape of when I called in and said there was anger in my voice, adding, "I would have done the same thing you did." Then he said he had to impose a 30-day suspension but would remove it if there were no other incidents within a year. However racism was so rampant from police officers up through the ranks that it was creating a mounting level of anxiety and anger in me. The incident with my racist neighbor brought all of this to the fore.

As soon as my leg healed, I was taken out of juvenile and put in robbery. There had never been a Black person assigned to robbery before me. They put me in charge of the gun control unit. There were about 300 guns that needed processing when I arrived. I had to contact the national crime information center and run the guns through the records of the Bureau of Alcohol, Tobacco, Firearms and Explosives (ATF). I was already behind when I started, because I didn't know how to process the guns—no one had trained me. I sought out an officer in auto theft who taught me how to process the guns in the system, and about two weeks later I had cleaned up all of the records.

When the sergeant showed up and asked, "How did you get all these guns done so quickly?"

I said, "I used the teletype system."

And he replied, "I didn't know you knew how to use the teletype system."

"Well, you never asked me," I answered.

One day, I had to go to court, and it just so happens that there was a Black court clerk there who asked, "Do you have your detective report with you?"

I said, "No, I don't know how to do that and didn't know I needed to have it." I told her that when I went to court with white officers and they had these well-typed reports, I just thought they were smart, and then she showed me how to produce the documents. My fellow officers in robbery didn't like the fact that I was becoming trained in all these procedures. There was continual suspicion directed towards me.

When I got back from court that day my sergeant looked at me and said, "Why did it take you so long?"

I said, "You can't rush the judge and you're called when you're called."

He said that when they sent me out, they didn't want me "messing around" and then brought me into the interrogation office with another officer, turned the light on over my head and started belittling me. "You might have been a good patrol officer, but you're not a pimple on a detective's badge."

It was 4:30 and my shift was over, so I stood up. He said, "Your day ends when I tell you." They berated me for fifteen more minutes then said, "You're free to go." I had some reports that needed filed, and then as I walked through the echoing halls of the jail—I heard the distinctive footsteps of the officer who had mocked and belittled me so extremely. I took out my weapon and aimed it—ready to blow his head off. But an image of Maria and the kids came in front of my eyes, and I paused long enough for him to turn the corner. A Black officer saw me standing there and said, "What's wrong? You look weird."

I said, "I almost shot Davis."

I turned in my badge and gun and came back Monday morning. But, as I was waiting to see the chief, a PSA airliner and a small Cessna collided over North Park, an area of San Diego. Everyone was killed as well as several people on the ground. I was told by the personnel officer to call in all officers who were off duty. After several hours of calling (on a rotary phone—this is before push-buttons or cell phones), I was assigned to the front desk while everyone worked the crash. And that's where I stayed after the crash too.

I handled complaints from citizens that had gone through city hall. Ninety-three of the complaints that were in the log book hadn't been followed up on, so I started to do just that. Most of the complaints were from Blacks and Mexicans.

As I worked on the complaints, trying to resolve them, I started getting physical threats against my life through my personal post office box. The captain said to give the letters to him, but I never heard anything further from him. He added, "You've cleaned up your act, but we are keeping our eyes on you."

I desperately needed to get away. I went into my watch commander and said, "I need a vacation."

He told me that he couldn't spare me, but I replied that if I got shot he could spare me then. Then he said, "OK, how long do you need?"

I said, "Three weeks." I took $3,000 out of the bank, got in my car and started driving. I didn't pack any clothes with me. I just drove, for

144

eight hours straight. Feeling sweaty and tired, I pulled over to buy a new outfit at a Montgomery Ward's and then went to a hotel.

It was the beginning of the end for me in the police force. I couldn't take it anymore. On my return, I quit.

I eventually got a lawyer to sue SDPD. My primary issue was the effect my knee injury had on my work. The knee would not heal properly. SDPD would not let me go out on patrol nor allow me to get promoted. I was continually doing menial tasks.

I won my case, though they fought it hard and had undercover officers following me throughout the investigation and court process.

— 21 —

On to Teaching

While I was a police officer I had the opportunity to finish college. I had AS and AA degrees, but I wanted to finish my bachelor's degree and go on to my master's. By that time, a university had started up for working people—National University, at one time the third largest private university in California. I finished my degree in public administration with an emphasis on criminology. I was thinking about becoming a counselor, so I started my master's in psychology.

One day I went out to intercept the president of the university on his morning walk and said, "Good morning. Do you mind if I walk with you?"

He replied, "This is my private time."

I said, "I realize that, but this is important." I asked him for a job.

After listening to me, the president said, "I want you to come up to the office with me to my morning meeting." He introduced me to deans and vice presidents and said, "I like the way he talks, what he stands for, and his demeanor," and then said to the vice president, "I want you to find a place for him." So, I was hired that morning and began working in admissions, researching transcripts and entering data. I was so happy working on campus and dressing up that I worked overtime every week for no additional pay.

I stayed in my position at National University for a little over a year, going into 1980-81. My job was to recruit for the university and make a Marine base satellite site successful. My duties for the university included publicity, office hours, and holding meetings with Admiral

Thomson. Once the university site was settled, we had an office party at my office, and the university chef prepared a wonderful meal. The admiral was the guest of honor, and we talked about what we wanted to do for the sailors on base and courses we could offer that would be of interest. Each course lasted a month, and students could do a year's work in 12 months by taking 12 different classes. Students could start fresh or enter as transfer students. It was geared toward military individuals who had started their degree but not finished or who were working adults and wanted to get a college degree. I understood the dynamics of the students entering the college, having lived through the same thing myself, and this made me a good recruiter. As I learned later, the president of the university was a retired naval officer, which fueled his desire to open the doors of education for enlisted men and women.

I was blossoming and feeling optimistic about my future, when, in 1981, I received a letter in the mail from the Board of Education telling me that I was recommended to teach a course at a high school. The letter suggested if I wanted the job, to come in for an interview. I was so happy at my present job, though, that I didn't pay much attention to it. And then, one day, the principal of a high school called me and asked if I had received his letter. Somewhat embarrassed that I had never responded to him, I went down and interviewed with him for a teaching position. He offered me the job. I asked for some time to consider it and went back to my campus to tell them the news. The president of National University said, "Go for it." And I did.

The school didn't have the curriculum for the course they wanted me to teach, and I had just a week to get everything prepared. I had to do all the administration work as well as write the lesson plans and content. It helped that I already had community college teaching credentials for life in the areas of human behavior and police science. I had achieved this in my last days as a police officer through the University of California, LA satellite courses. I wasn't certified to teach K-12, so I had to take an education law test that was 5 hours long. It was a pass or fail test, and I passed it. I was certified and got my K-12 teaching credentials.

I started out two hours per day, teaching the Regional Occupation Program (ROP). The class was an elective for high school juniors and seniors and was also open for adults to come into the high school to take the class. I taught human behavior, psychology and a lot of information about law enforcement. My motivation was to inspire students to become probation counselors and go into law. I wasn't as interested in inspiring them to be police officers or correctional officers as I had seen too much corruption in those fields.

I kept my class interesting by inviting a lot of guest speakers, including lawyers and police officers who were good with both school kids and civilians. The school that I began working at was Samuel E. Morse High School, which at that time, was a thoroughly integrated school with about 1/3 Hispanic, 1/3 Black and 1/3 white students. Because I was teaching an ROP course, students could also bus in from other high schools to take my course. So, I had a good mixture of students and even some adults. I styled the whole curriculum with a syllabus and course work, like a first-year college course. My standards were quite high, and my demands were patterned somewhat after Marine Corps training.

I was strict, but fair.

The first semester at Morse High School went well, though it was a little like on-the-job training for me. It was important to me to dress the part, and I wore a suit every day with a magenta carnation. Most importantly, I built a good rapport with students (with only a few exceptions) and with colleagues. My program was so successful that the district widened it to three high schools, and I had more mileage clocked than any other teacher in the district, with over 100 miles traveled each month. Morse High School, where I had begun the program, was in a predominantly Black community, and it had been difficult to get enough kids interested in the course to make it successful, so, instead, I was sent out to white schools, where students seemed more interested in the "law & order" aspect of the class. My class periods were staggered so I would have 1st and 2nd at one school, 4th and 5th at another, and 6th period at the last school. I would start at Patrick Henry High School, next to Mira Mesa High School, then end the day at Serra High School. I did get a few students from a Black school that

bused in to take my class—two were from Lincoln High School, the "Blackest" school in the heart of the Black and Mexican community. One of these students became a lawyer; he played baseball and got a scholarship to college. The other became a legal secretary.

At this time, I had so many hours that I had a full-time teaching contract. Parents were satisfied with the program, and several graduates became dog catchers, probation officers, and police officers.

Teaching for the Regional Occupational Program.

In the third year of teaching the course, I added another part to the curriculum—training students to become private security officers. I taught six hours in the day and then an hour at night for the security officer preparatory course. I was extremely busy, teaching seven hours a day and doing all the prep work and grading of assignments and tests.

A few students are indelibly engraved on my memory for distinctly different reasons. One of my students, Gregory, went on to finish college and became a teacher at Patrick Henry High School while I was still teaching there. Another student, Robin, had anxiety problems. I talked with Robin and gained her respect. One day, she came to me and blurted out, "I know why I have such a big butt."

I was startled but said, "You do?"

Robin said she was going through her grandma's attic and found a picture of a Black man and asked her grandma who he was, and was told it was her grandfather. Robin appeared white, but apparently, she had a Black grandfather in her ancestry.

One day I gave a student called James an individual assignment in class, and he told me, "Fuck you, Mr. Wilkerson." I quickly grabbed a meter stick and smacked him on his rear end. Realizing what I had done, I immediately became scared of the consequences. I went to the principal, and he called the student's mother, who was single.

She said, "Good. Any time you need to, swat him on the butt!" But it scared me so much I knew I would never do it again.

An adult woman, Cindy, is also a memorable student. I told my students to take notes in my class, and at times I would collect the notes to see how well they were paying attention. I suggested that it might even get them an extra point on their grades if they were taking thorough notes. I was amazed that Cindy would even record oral pauses—and every little thing that I said—in her notes. She was an A student and became a security officer after she graduated.

One of my students became pregnant at 16 and had to petition the school to continue taking classes. They put her in my class, and she asked why the baby couldn't come with her. I told her that they didn't allow babies in class, but maybe she could get that policy changed. So, I went with her to the school board and she pushed it all the way through, until by the next school semester the district introduced child-care for students. This helped teenage mothers to graduate high school and made an enormous difference.

Teaching really helped me transition to civilian life, helped me transition from my former military and police department roles and modes of thinking, and was the career in which I felt most fulfilled.

— 22 —

Robyn and Tedd

When I began working for National University as a counselor for admissions and acquired my own office, we gave a buffet luncheon open to the public to attract likely students to courses in business, community and military. The buffet was for working adults who wanted to further their education. We had a luncheon every Sunday, and I made sure it was a first class affair.

One Sunday, a potential student brought her friend to the luncheon. Claire was the student interested in enrolling, and her friend Robyn, who she brought along, was white, blonde, and attractive and was dressed as though she had just come from church. Later Claire told me that Robyn was interested in me. My first impression was that she looked good and seemed nice.

We met a few times to see where it might go. I took her out to breakfast to one of my favorite spots near the ocean, to a French restaurant. She read the menu and said, "I don't see anything I want, so why don't you order for me."

I ordered Eggs Benedict, not knowing that she had never had eggs that way before. When it came, she said, "What's this?" She didn't like it because the eggs were over-easy, refused to eat it, and only drank her coffee.

After each of our dates, she went back home. I didn't ask why she never invited me over, because I was raised to respect women and give them the space or privacy they needed. It was my understanding that Robyn was single, because she presented herself that way. I was divorced and available. However, as it turned out—she was married. Unfortunately, I wouldn't find this out until much later.

Robyn would come by my apartment from time to time, and we continued to go out on dates occasionally. Finally, on Labor Day, I decided to make my move and see if we could be more serious. I got all dressed up because she was coming over, and I anticipated taking her out to dinner. But when she got there, she said she didn't want to go out to dinner and just wanted to go to bed! I wasn't complaining. Not knowing what to say, I said OK.

Three hours later she left.

After a while, I started to become more suspicious of why she never invited me over to her place. Through my police contacts, I found out where Robyn lived. I drove by her house, and my first thought was that it looked like too much house for a single, young female working as a hairstylist. So, I asked Claire if Robyn was married. Claire held out for a while, because she was really good friends with Robyn, but after I pressed her repeatedly, eventually she said, "Yes, Robyn's married."

One day Claire asked me to come over for dinner at her house. I was kind of suspicious of this, because I didn't know which woman to trust at this point. But, I went over to Claire's for dinner and enjoyed the food. She warmed up over dinner and told me that Robyn's husband was in the Marine Corps and was white. I became alarmed and scared. Dating a white female was risky enough but to cross a white woman's white husband—a military man—was something I would never have done if I had known everything up front.

I confronted Robyn by letter asking about her behavior and the entire situation. She responded with silence. I had already crossed a huge line by dating and being intimate with her, so cutting things off didn't entirely solve the situation. Robyn said she was in divorce proceedings. I asked how long that had been going on, and she said since just before she met me. I tucked this into the back of my mind, although I didn't fully trust her word on anything at this point. I had to extract bits and pieces of information from Robyn and then confirm things by talking to Claire, to see if both women were giving me the same response.

I asked Robyn how long her husband had been in the Marine Corps, and she said, "Fifteen years." I thought, "Dang." I asked her what was going to happen next with her divorce proceedings, and she said she was going to expedite it. I asked her why, and she said, "Because I'm pregnant." I almost jumped out of my skin! I knew she had seen other men, but I thought she hadn't seen anyone since meeting me. I asked Claire and she confirmed this.

Robyn had stopped eating and was wearing a girdle to hide her pregnancy from her husband. I wasn't close enough to Robyn at this point to know exactly what she was doing on a daily basis while she was pregnant, but I knew she smoked and wasn't eating well. I didn't know if she doing anything else that might be harmful to the baby. Meantime, her husband Dennis had orders to Okinawa, and she chose not to go.

I was on Robyn's case about smoking while pregnant. After her husband was deployed overseas, I even followed her to work one day and saw her smoking a cigarette as I was passing her on the interstate. I glared at her, and when she saw me she was so startled that she almost wrecked her car. I didn't follow her anymore. I was worried every day about my child, and how I could find a positive outcome to all of this. And it was obvious. I was in trouble again because of my naivety with regards women.

When Tedd was born on June 19, 1981, he was underweight and had to have a blood transfusion. Later, he was a special needs child going into school, because he had some attention problems. This made me even more upset about Robyn's poor care of her body during the pregnancy, because of the effect on an innocent child.

———— ♦ ————

Robyn and I were not interacting at all romantically anymore; in fact, the tension over the hidden marriage and surprise pregnancy killed any sort of attraction that was initially there. However, I was constantly thinking about the baby. I visited Robyn sometimes at her home when her husband was overseas. I found out that she had left school early, because she didn't like it.

After the baby was born and Dennis was back from deployment, it turned out that Dennis was happy about her having a baby. It turned out they were NOT in divorce proceedings and never had been.

My son was born at the Naval hospital, and I wanted to see him—to see what he looked like—and then I planned on leaving everything alone if she was going to stay married. I told Elton to bring a police camera—a Polaroid—to take a picture of the baby. He said that he couldn't do that! I said, "Yes you can." I was desperate; because this might be the only time that I laid eyes on my child. So, he checked out the camera.

When we got there, I asked the nurse to point out the baby to me, claiming we were related. She took us to the room and pointed to the middle of the room and said, "The one right there in the middle." It was hard to see much of him, because he was all bundled up and his eyes were closed. I put my hands on the glass and said, "If you feel my spirit, open your eyes." And this little baby opened his eyes. I was over-whelmed and promised that I would stay in his life as much as I could and for as long as possible.

Robyn dropped by my work to show me the baby and told me they had named him Theodore. Although I liked seeing little Tedd, I felt extremely uncomfortable. I didn't know what frame of mind her husband was in and if he was following her or what. So, I decided to go meet Robyn's mother. I told her, "I'm here to ask you to tell your daughter to leave me alone."

The next thing to do was to contact Dennis. I called him and said, "I don't want to cause any harm or cause problems for you or your wife. My only concern is the child."

He said that he appreciated me calling. "You don't have to worry;

I'll take care of this baby as if he's my own." So, I thought, "Wow. Either this guy is crazy or is just a really good white man."

Later, Robyn and family moved onto the base, but Robyn didn't like being around military wives and wanted to move off base again. She contacted me and said she was going back to work when Tedd was two months old, and she said she needed a babysitter. She asked if Marcia would babysit Tedd while she worked because she needed childcare. Unbeknownst to me, Robyn and Marcia had met somehow through Claire, and she said that they got along well. Marcia was living at home with her mother, and I thought that babysitting would not be cool with Maria. But, Maria didn't mind, because she told Marcia it wasn't the baby's fault. So, for the first six months of his life, Tedd went to Maria's, where Marcia babysat him.

When Dennis found out Robyn was working and putting the baby in childcare, he confronted her and asked where Tedd was and who was taking care of him. He was furious that she was having my daughter Marcia take care of Tedd, and their marriage began falling apart even more than it had before.

Robyn decided to leave Dennis and had Marcia help her move off the base while Dennis was at work.

Things were a mess. I felt out of control of the situation. My job and my health began falling apart. I couldn't sleep and started having problems focusing on things. I contacted Robyn and told her it was all really bothering me.

She said, "I'm sorry, but what are you going to do about it?"

I said I was concerned about her and Tedd. She was now physically separated from her husband but still not divorced. So, I got an apartment and we moved in together, but it didn't last. It didn't feel good, because Robyn and I weren't married, and Mark especially started resenting it. He felt like he was being displaced by another son. I didn't know what to do with Mark's emotions, my own feelings, and the fact that the relationship wasn't working out anyways. So, we split up yet again. Tedd was 10 months old at that time. I would keep him on the weekends, which I loved, while she was working at her hairstyling job.

———◆———

Eventually, however, to give Tedd my last name, Robyn and I got married by a minister who was an acquaintance of mine. He married us in his little church on a Sunday in La Jolla. We invited Robyn's mother and my kids, but no one showed up. By this time, Tedd was four years old. Robyn and I continued to have an on again off again relationship for some years.

I wanted Robyn to get enrolled in a community college, which she did against her own wishes. She got good grades at first but later dropped out. She was an excellent house cleaner—like Maria—and kept herself clean and organized. However, she couldn't cook very well and I tried to teach her, but it didn't work out. I would get dressed up and take her out, but again it was me running things as I did in my first marriage. It became abundantly clear that we had nothing in common. I kept telling myself, "You did it for the child," but I was miserable being with her.

Unbeknownst to me, Robyn started having an affair with a white man who had a place on the Colorado River, and she left one weekend saying she was just going to hang out with some friends. She stayed away much longer than a weekend.

I became suspicious and moved out. I had had enough.

Robyn told me that she was moving in with this man whose name was Dick. As it turned out, he was married, and she moved in with him and his wife. I felt like that it was not a good situation for Tedd. They lived in San Carlos, a suburb of San Diego and Robyn put Tedd in the local elementary school primarily for white kids. I visited the school one day and noticed that he was sitting quietly in a corner, all by himself. I asked why he was in the corner and the teacher said he liked it there, but I knew better because Tedd liked people and children and was usually full of energy. He wasn't learning.

I went back to the school to get a progress report. The counselor, a Black lady, said, "I understand that you are Tedd's father, and Tedd is having some problems in school."

Between the counselor and me, we got Tedd re-designated as "Black" to qualify him for Title IX assistance. She said that Robyn and Dick never came to visit him at school, so it would be nice if I came to visit him in class sometimes. I was there 57 times that year, and the school started calling me the Classroom Dad.

Tedd was in third grade but hadn't started reading so he was way behind. I got phonics books and started teaching Tedd on my own. I took him to libraries. He loved it and would go through book after book once he learned to read.

I felt as though I was beginning to achieve more expertise in being a father which I had unfortunately struggled with before.

— 23 —

Amy

While I was teaching at Patrick Henry High School, I met Amy. One morning we both happened to be in the mailroom. She said, "Good morning Mr. Wilkerson," and then asked me if I would come to speak in her class about the ROP program sometime.

"Sure," I said, "but you'll have to contact me later because the bell is about to ring." I was always at my door promptly, because I greeted every student as they came inside. As I dashed off to my bungalow classroom, I kept thinking, "Who was that lady?" Her appearance with her long skirt and boots and her foreign accent made me think she was unusual for a high school teacher. I kept wondering if her accent was English or Scottish.

A full year later, my schedule had changed a bit, and I was at Serra High School. Again, I saw Amy there. She said, "What are you doing here?" She had been transferred to Serra to teach Video Production and English. At Serra, there were more Black kids because it was near a Navy housing area. At this school, every teacher had to pick a committee to be on. At the beginning of the school year I had selected Human/Race Relations. It turned out that she was the school liaison and headed that committee, so we started seeing each other more.

That year, we had a Christmas party at Serra, and although I went, it was just too boring. A few of the other teachers agreed—the dancing was boring, the music was boring. I said, "I'm going to the Yacht Club," which was a popular San Diego night club.

Amy didn't want to stay at the party either, and she rode with me to the club. It was about 9 or 10 at night by the time we arrived, and boy was it jam-packed with live dancing. It was so packed that we couldn't get a table, so we just started dancing. I had on dark green trousers and a red sweater that night, and Amy wore black pants and a red sweater. She looked considerably better than when I first met her, and I said to myself, "Wow, she can dance!" Thankfully, by that time I could dance too.

I remember while "Feliz Navidad" was playing, I started singing the song to her, and we were laughing. At about 2 a.m., we left to go home and as we were walking down the boardwalk, she slipped her arm through mine. I dropped her off back where the school party was held—where she had left her car, and she kissed me on the cheek and said, "I'll see you next year!" It was the holiday break, so next year was only a week away.

We didn't see each other until after school resumed. We were back in the grind of work and bumped into each other when we had committee meetings and school activities. Amy and I got to know each other through our work on the Race/Human Relations committee, and the committee planned days where teachers would have half day in-service training. Then we spent more extended time together. I noticed that Amy started dressing really sharp, wearing nicer clothes and suits. She was MCing an in-service event one time, and I began thinking to myself that she was different from other teachers, different from the white teachers, and different from the Black teachers too. She cared about kids, needy kids and kids of color. I started feeling like we had a lot in common, but at this time I still didn't have any interest in her romantically.

We had known each other for two years before we ever dated, and in the third year we would do so many things at school together that we began doing things after school with each other too. During our third spring break, we decided to take a trip together to New Mexico. I told her to bring warm clothes—because I knew we were going to the mountains, and it would be cold. We enjoyed each other on the trip.

At the wedding.

She loved to laugh, and she played cribbage. I even told her way back then, "I'm going to write a book someday."

Things progressed and eventually we decided to get married.

We had a beautiful wedding with an African drummer and Scottish bagpipes. We decided to get married on a Monday and we got married the following Friday, on June 26th, 1992. We were both teaching summer school, but within the five days of our "engagement," we organized everything for the wedding. I had a minister friend who administered the vows, and we held the ceremony at my good friend Francisco's house, with the ceremony outside, under a gazebo. We told as many friends and my fellow Black police officers as we could, so we would have some guests at the wedding. We had the first Black chief, Roulette, of the SDPD there. We had teachers and a few other friends, and Tedd attended our wedding. He loved the apple cider and convinced himself that he was drunk on it.

Francisco cooked a whole meal for our wedding guests, and we had champagne. We had the bagpiper pipe us in as we walked in on the path under fruit trees—figs, oranges, and avocados. We had a professor of music from San Diego University play African drums. I had a suit on with a kente cloth around my neck, and Amy wore a nice cream-colored dress. We walked together all the way up to the minister.

160

When we got there, I said, "I forgot."

The minister said, "What did you forget?"

I said, "I never asked her to marry me!" I was trying to add some humor into the moment, so I asked Amy, "Will you marry me?" and she said, "Yes."

I told Amy's son, Douglas, who attended, "Welcome to the family," and he said, "I don't know about family, but I thought it was about time I attended one of her weddings." Amy and I both had previous marriages that hadn't worked out well, so not everyone had the highest hopes for our union lasting.

The day that we got married, Amy and I went to our separate houses after the wedding. The government had garnished my wages and charged me back taxes that I didn't owe, but I couldn't afford an attorney to fight it. With few choices, I had asked my ex-wife, Maria, if I could rent a bedroom from her, so when Amy and I got married, and I had Tedd for the weekend, I went to my room with Tedd, and Amy went to her own house. It was not ideal.

Soon after our wedding, we made arrangements to move in together. I loved to cook, and I found out that she wasn't that great of a cook. I primarily did the cooking and, after dinner, we would often play cribbage to relax, or simply sit and philosophize about our students (we had some of the same students) and had a lot of great discussions about them.

One year, she had a whole class of football players in her English class, so I showed up to help her get them all in line. She also taught video production, and I thought that was really neat. We had rich kids as well as students living in poverty, so we would create programs to include all the kids from diverse backgrounds. One year, Amy came up with a senior program that was a Medieval Faire. We had it in the school wrestling room, which was decorated to look like a great hall. Unfortunately all the decorations in the world could not take care of the body odors and she said, "I'll never do this again in here with 'teenage male funk' smelling up the place."

The next year we took the Medieval Faire outside. The Defense Department had a lot of air and space events at a nearby park, so we staged the Faire at the park. Even the tall, skinny, Black principal dressed up as a medieval character. When I saw him, I started laughing. He said, "Mr. Wilkerson, why are you laughing?"

I said, "You look like a medieval pimp!"

Amy rented costumes for the students who had been voted as "royalty" but who couldn't afford costumes. We both did a lot to show our students that we were teachers that cared.

I started a club called New Horizons with a Black female teacher, and we mostly had Black students with a couple Hispanic and white kids. This was a club mostly for students who needed opportunities. I had started another group called Serra Men of Quality (SMQ) targeted at Black boys, because the white boys had their clubs and the Hispanic boys did too.

Later, when my teaching position was closed out, and I became a school police officer, no other Black men who worked there stepped up to the plate to carry on the club. I had to get special permission to continue to work with these young Black males. Because no one else would volunteer, Amy became the official faculty advisor for the club and conducted meetings when I could not make it.

These activities really bonded us together and built the foundation for our relationship. Meeting Amy and having a female that I was equal to, who was secure in her person, was like a new chapter of my life opened up, and with it, many happy moments and companionship. It was the first time that I was in a relationship where there was a friendship that set the tone and foundation of our interactions. I was really good friends with Amy even before we got married, and our friendship solidified our love for each other. I didn't have to take care of her, and she was constantly showing me that she was assertive and self-sufficient. I learned in time that she had survived her own fair share of troubles in life, which gave her practice in problem solving and made her less fragile and more empathetic than most women I had known.

Traveling with Amy was a lot of fun. We went to Great Britain a couple of times, and I met my father-in-law and her family. We were young and traveled well together. We were flexible, and were making enough money to allow us to enjoy ourselves. We made about $150,000 a year between the two of us, and that was quite a bit back then. I had always been in the mode of trying to take care of someone or save the world, just trying to do the right thing in the neighborhood, so-to-speak. She hadn't gotten out and experienced a fun life either, so we both had a wonderful time traveling and exploring together.

However, when we visited Las Vegas on one of our trips, we were accosted on the street by two white males. They dashed ice from a cooler at us as their truck speed toward us, yelling racial profanities. This prompted us to not hold hands in public. Amy couldn't believe some of the ways we were treated, because racism wasn't the same in Scotland, and she hadn't been with a Black man before me.

In one restaurant that we went to in Del Mar, we had a wonderful view of the setting sun. We placed our order for drinks, got them, but the waitress never came back to take our order for a meal. As we waited, we became aware of a very elderly white male staring at us. (This was a usual experience). Eventually he got up and made his way towards us in a very shaky manner as his wife implored him to come back to their table. In a trembling voice he explained to us that he was not staring at us but at the sunset. It was odd, to say the least, but more importantly it was now over an hour, and we had still not ordered. There was clearly an issue as the waitress ignored any attempt to have her come to our table. We decided to leave. On the way out we asked for the manager and explained the situation with the waitress. His response, "Oh, we've had problems with her before." We turned down an offer for a meal voucher. We had no intention of returning.

Sometimes the degree to which strangers stared at us was funny. In a Vietnamese restaurant in Hillcrest we were enjoying our meal when a very tall young man came in to pick up a take-out dinner. He was so busy staring on the way out that he walked in to the low-hanging chandelier!

The two of us went to happy hours and danced, went to plays and did a lot of fun things together. In my previous relationships, Maria didn't like going out much at all and never seemed to enjoy it if I convinced her to try. Robyn was never completely relaxed on the dance floor. Amy was just the opposite. She had rhythm and loved to dance. She would say, "Let's go; let's go; let's do it!" to most any new adventure or chance to enjoy life. Amy has been a really good mate and companion for me.

Albert and Amy at the Marine Corps Ball on the RMS Queen Mary in Long Beach, CA.

But at times, my relationship with Amy was somewhat strained by the custody situation I had to manage with Tedd. When I found out that Dick wasn't just a boyfriend but was married and dating Robyn openly, it just didn't set right with me. I went to court many times due to my concerns with what was going on in Dick and Robyn's household—uncomfortable with Tedd being part of the living arrangement of Robyn, Dick and his wife, who was his former sister-in-law. Tedd had even asked me at one time, "How many people can sleep in one bed?"

I answered, "That depends on the size of the bed."

In court, Robyn swore nothing kinky was going on, and, I couldn't prove anything. Although I was going for sole custody, I also didn't want to take Tedd away entirely from his mother. We had joint legal custody, but she had physical custody, and I had visitation every other weekend and holidays. Robyn was now living in Blythe CA, a long way from San Diego. Every other weekend, she was supposed to bring Tedd to me, but, in effect, that never happened. So, the judge said to meet halfway between San Diego and Blythe but that didn't work either. Every other weekend I would drive all the way to pick him up and all the way back. For seven years, I drove 430 miles round trip *twice* each weekend to be with him—going to pick him up on a Friday and taking him back on Sunday. In addition, I would take a sick day to go to his school meetings to make sure he was doing OK.

One time driving Tedd back, I had a heart attack. I knew I didn't feel well so I went straight to the hospital in Blythe. This was my second heart attack. (The first one was in 1995). The hospital confirmed I had had a heart attack and flew me back to a San Diego hospital, and I left behind Amy's sports car that I had driven over to the desert. I had to inform the hospital that I had weapons in the car and showed them my credentials. Amy and Mark drove back out to the desert to pick up her car.

I was under stress and duress looking out for Tedd. I knew that I would give my life for him but also knew that I couldn't keep up the driving back and forth without some intervention. It was a hardship on me and on Amy to have these long trips, because she was worried about my health and me driving across the desert when it was 110 degrees.

I did as much as I could for Tedd. Amy also did a lot for Tedd, though Robyn and Dick told Tedd that stepmothers were mean and would never take loving care of him. Nonetheless, we found ways to get over that and have some good times. But having a blended family with my kids and Amy's kids was like flying an airplane while you're building it.

I did the best I could but it wasn't perfect.

— 24 —

Temecula

When we first moved to this upscale place, there were 30,000 people in Temecula, now it's over 100,000. We loved it, because it wasn't the big city or the country—although we had an hour commute to work, on a good traffic day.

Amy and I bought our first house together in Temecula. It was a really nice house with four bedrooms and 2,400 square feet. It was the first time either of us had ever lived a comfortable life like this. I thought, "You have kids and I have kids; let's do the Brady Bunch thing." Looking back on this time, I was in denial about the potential complications and naively thought that we could have a great blended family with everyone getting along well. However, with all of our children now being adults and gone from home, we never even got all of them at our house at one time. They all had their own lives, and it never seemed to work out. My idea of filling a dream house with a blended family for holidays and special occasions popped like cheap bubble gum. Although our kids rarely came to visit, I enjoyed the experience of having a nice space to share with Amy. It was the first time I really enjoyed living with another person.

———◆———

It was clear by the end of a year that this would just be a big empty dream house with a lot of unused space. It was beautiful, but it was not bustling with activity. We had two cars, a pickup truck, leased corrals for two horses at the neighboring ranch, and even had a comma in our

Riding his Tennessee Walker, Joy (17 hands), for the first time in Temecula.

checking account. I thought I would never be able to afford a house that cost even $30,000. But, having done that for Maria, I knew I could attain a higher goal this time. Our first home in Temecula was $200,000, which blew my mind.

Then land developers started a new housing development next to where we lived, and I would stop by and look at the models of the homes. I thought, wow—I LOVE this house! I said, this is how I want to live. The model I loved had 3,500 square feet, a wine cellar, and all these extras. We put all our finances together and qualified to start building. However, once they started building, and we had sold our first Temecula home, the property developer flaked out and the completion date for the house moved off in to the uncertain future! We became homeless as we waited for our new home—moving in to Francisco's house in San Diego while he was gone overseas.

With this new, bigger house, we weren't trying to just keep up

with the Joneses; we were going to be living better than the Joneses!
I was there when they made the curved stairway right on the property. I was fascinated by the artistry, how they shaped the wood
with steam and finished it. It was so beautiful. We put a baby grand
piano on lay-away and started buying a ton of furniture for the bedrooms, bathrooms, formal dining room and two living rooms. We
had TV's in multiple rooms. Talk about materialistic; we were going
for it! We were ready once the house was finished and moved all the
furniture in.

One day when my mom visited, she was so happy about the house
that she was bouncing down the stairs on her rear end going "Whee,
whee!" and said, "I've never known a relative to have such a house!" This
really pleased me.

———◆———

After I retired from teaching, I began to develop a catering business in Temecula. This had been successful as a part-time venture
in San Diego but would it work there to the north, in Riverside
County?

I had started catering in 1995, cooking for events, helping restaurants and organizations with food, but now I decided to go ahead and
get started on my own. I ordered a cooker from Michigan and went to
look at it before they shipped it out. The manufacturer didn't have all
the items I wanted built onto it, so they adapted the cooker for me and
shipped it. To get started in Temecula I got my food handler's card,
license and insurance. I leased kitchen space from a restaurant and
would use some of the restaurant's equipment once they closed in the
evening.

My catering business was set up to be on-site service. Some things
needed prepped in advance, but all the cooking was done at the event's
location. I spent about $20,000 in equipment and decided to do
western-style barbeque. I named my business Sgt. Wilkie's Southwest
Catering Company and put on a grand opening, renting a space and

Catering for 1,500 people at a cancer benefit with longtime friend, Francisco.

inviting friends and family members and other people we had met in Temecula. It was a nice affair; we had about 50 people come out, and everyone was excited about my food.

I started getting jobs through word of mouth and began advertising locally. I joined the tourist's association in the town. The Old Town of Temecula was western-themed, so my business fit in well. Any time the town had fairs and activities, I set up to promote my catering. I would go to things like hotrod and motorcycle shows with my BBQ, especially in the spring and summer—but not so much in the winter, when it was cold.

Temecula held a hot-air balloon festival, and I would have my barbeque for sale there. I did beach weddings, military events and all kinds of catering within 100 miles of Temecula. Business got pretty good, and I was able to pay off all my equipment within a brief period. We had a lot of ranch parties as well, and any friends who were getting married would call and ask me to cater their weddings.

I catered country affairs, some of which proved to be unique experiences. One of these parties really scared me. It was for a motorcycle gang that looked like Hell's Angels, and was held in a very remote area, nestled in the hills near Temecula. I wore all my western clothes to try to fit in, and, luckily, the folks were warm toward me—maybe the kegs of beer being consumed helped the situation!

One of my large events was a benefit for a victim of cancer, where I served 1,500 people. The day before, the Mekeel Ranch, where we kept our horses, had a Black Angus steer that they slaughtered for this event—its name was Archer. I prepared all the food, including Archer's 1,400 pounds of beef. I also cooked a hog that weighed 250 pound, but cooking a whole steer and a hog presented a challenge for oven space, so I got creative and built a huge pit, 8x4x5 feet, wrapping the seasoned meat up in foil—even burying the beans, and cooked it all for 24 hours.

There were 500 motorcycles that came out to this cancer benefit. Most people rode double, making the attendance about 1,000—with another 500 people arriving in cars. I think adrenaline carried me through the prep and serving of this massive endeavor. I was excited about the cause and thrilled that my cooking talent could contribute in a positive way to help a cancer victim. It went off really well, and I only charged the organization for the supplies and not for my time. Archer the steer was also donated, and I'm sure they made quite a lot in proceeds.

I was there working for 24 hours straight but somehow was still functioning and standing—probably my military training kicking in to complete my mission. The day of the event, I was so tired when I got home that I fell asleep sitting in a lawn chair in my garage in front of the open garage door and woke up the following morning!

The benefit was for a specific cancer patient, and at the time I never thought I would have the same type of cancer as the man who benefited from this cookout. Now that I, too, am fighting this disease, knowing I helped him feels good.

I have many fond memories of other events we catered as well, including providing for one of the Rose Parade entries. We hosted a team called the Heinz Hitch, for the Heinz food corporation. They came from Pennsylvania and had the wonderful Percheron horses (one of the largest draft horses in the world) as their team. The Heinz staff

Albert goofing around on a Heinz Hitch Percheron of 19 hands at Mekeel Ranch.

would get to the Mekeel Ranch a week or two before Christmas to do the training for the horses and prepare for the event, and we threw them a big party after the parade was complete. We catered this event for three years, and I loved the connection of the horses to my catering business.

− 25 −

School Policing

After living in Temecula for a while, the catering company had not built up in the way I had hoped. Our mortgage was high, and, in addition, I began growing a little restless. I sat somewhat bored in our beautiful, new home: the house with the turret and leaded glass windows in the circular entrance way and the hand-crafted—curving staircase, etc. It was beautiful, but I was bored watching TV at home, alone, (Amy was still teaching in San Diego and commuting). Then a notice came in the mail that they needed police officers in the schools.

I applied, and it came back that I was number one for the campus police officer position and number two at the patrol position. I didn't want patrol, so I went down to apply for the school police officer position. I had my current background check, lie detector tests, and academy training. All I had to do was go through the requalification course for three weeks—the only problem that I had was any activity that put pressure on my knees.

Soon, I became a campus police officer at Lincoln High School. I had guessed that was where I would be assigned and told the police chief, "I'm going to Lincoln High School."

He said, "I don't know about that, but if you were going there it wouldn't be because you are Black."

I thought, "I don't know who you're fooling."

I said later to the Chief after I was assigned there, "Tom, tell me something. I want to know the truth. When you hired me for Lincoln, you said you weren't putting me there because I'm Black."

School police officer at Lincoln High School, San Diego City Schools.

He said, "I'm no fool. I wouldn't put a white person there."

Lincoln High School was the roughest school in San Diego. In addition to the normal school year, I worked summer school and drove with a detective, Carl, who was Black. We had good times together in the summer. I was also able to teach Community Policing and some other classes for officers from Southern California. These were all summer classes, so I didn't miss any work at school. I really loved teaching, and we were working with a department from Los Angeles whose school district had over 400 police officers. I enjoyed working with them and had a really good rapport. I didn't have significant problems with anything, although there were some people who were jealous of my academic degrees and higher qualifications.

As a school police officer, I was the only one qualified to be promoted to lieutenant. But, I didn't want to apply because I planned to do five years as a campus officer and then go back to retirement. And that's what I did. But some guys stayed on just to get the lieutenant badge, to feel the power of having that rank. I didn't want it, and the little bit of extra pay didn't mean that much to me either.

Just before I retired from the San Diego Unified School District for the second time, I had a heart attack due to the stress of working at

173

Lincoln High. I was arresting people every day, usually for drugs and weapons. One kid was involved in a homicide and someone sent him to Lincoln High even though he wasn't a student there. I heard all this running and yelling, and I ran down to the gymnasium. He had a gun, but we were able to apprehend him. This was the only gun I encountered, but there were a lot of knives and plenty of marijuana on campus. One girl, Tamiko, was Black and Japanese and I arrested her so many times that I actually got tired of it.

One day I arrived and saw Tamiko coming up through the alley, and said, "Give me your purse." She did, and she had four to five grams of marijuana in it. I arrested her for felony possession, and she never returned to school. The kids knew that I wasn't a bully, but I was fair and held them to the rules.

One day I broke up a party, and as I was in the process of this, a car drove up and pointed a laser at my chest. That really shook me up. It turned out that it was just a laser and not a gun. The kid was already on probation for shining a laser at an airplane, but this could have gone wrong in so many ways.

I enjoyed counseling at the school, which was needed on many occasions.

There were a brother and sister who were in special education. The boy really loved girls and started trying to get girls to interact physically with him. I went to his parents' house, and it turned out that they were over 300 pounds each and foster parents who were just sitting on the couch continually watching TV I reported that the state needed to investigate the family. Eventually, the boy reached up a girl's skirt. She screamed and ran away. I arrested him, but only because that was the only way he would receive counseling and psychological testing. I didn't want him to be labeled as a sex offender, because he had a mental issue, so I told the court that both kids needed counseling, and I was concerned about what might be going on at home.

I had another sex-related case. April was a biracial girl, really cute, and her parents had her when they were both 16 years old. Both of her parents would drive up to the school and drop her off. One day, I noticed she quickly disappeared. I followed her and saw that an older guy was picking her up at school after her parents dropped her off. The next thing I knew, I saw a boy walking around with a big video camera on his shoulder. He was showing everyone at the basketball game a sex tape of April. He had lured her to his house and had sex with her and taped it, without her knowing. The sex tape was played through the whole school before I caught onto it, and I told the student to take the video camera home or I would confiscate it. He didn't comply, so I took the camera and brought it into my office. I was shocked out of my mind when I saw what was on the tape. I brought the female vice principal into my office—we were called The Regulators at the school—and we went through the tape together to make sure no other students were involved.

I called the student into my office and read him his rights and arrested him for a sex crime. One of the office aides heard about it and called his mother, telling her that he was being arrested on false charges. When I heard this, I brought the aide into my office and told her she was not to come back on campus. People didn't like that, because she was the basketball coach's aide too, but I could not have anyone interfering with arrests or investigations.

We didn't handle rapes or homicides, so I called the San Diego Police Department and asked for a female officer who worked in sex crimes cases. I laid the story out and showed her the tape, and we interviewed April. She wouldn't say a word at first, but then she broke down and said that she had consented to sex, but she didn't want it taped—there was actually footage of her saying she didn't want it taped on the video.

————— ◆ —————

During my time at Lincoln High, I wanted to get rid of the metal hallway lockers but the principal didn't like me too much and wasn't listening to my suggestion. I proposed that removing the lockers would solve some of the problems with kids being tardy to class. The principal said students needed lockers to get their books to class, and I said they could use backpacks. He countered that he didn't think it would be good for their backs and that lockers were just a part of the high school experience. I dropped it, not wanting to argue with him and instead took my campaign to my coworkers. Eventually, I won out and the lockers were removed.

Every week, I had to write a report on graffiti and get it cleaned up. The school was 50% Mexican, and I could never catch a kid painting the graffiti, but I caught a few Mexican kids with graffiti in their notebooks. I told one of the kids named Hugo, "You know graffiti will get you kicked out of high school."

He said, "Mr. Wilkerson, don't you know this is art?"

I said, "But you're not in art class." By the time Hugo was 18, he was still a junior. He got kicked out of high school that year for graffiti.

———— ◆ ————

All this time, Amy and I were commuting with 1½ hours of traffic one way. We had to be at school at 7:30 in the morning, so we left before 6 a.m. I was always on call when we came into radio range, and we both had our own vehicles. By this time, Amy was going around to different schools as an itinerant Life Skills teacher after earning her master's degree. We always had a lot to discuss about our jobs—our work, our goals and what we were trying to accomplish in school.

However, the stress of my job finally really got to me, and I had the symptoms of a heart attack. It was in the morning. I was at home, ready to leave for work. I couldn't swallow; I started sweating and having chest pains. I told Amy my symptoms, and she took me straight to hospital. I was transferred to Scripps Hospital in San Diego, and after this I didn't go back to work. Three weeks later, when I could walk and drive again, I cleaned out my office at school and retired. Because I had been a teacher previously, I retired again with a teacher's pension.

About a year after I retired from school policing, we moved to Idaho.

My series of heart attacks was worrisome, because I had now survived several heart attacks but didn't know how many times it would take for one to be fatal. Eventually I had another heart attack when we were living in Idaho. I went to Sacred Heart hospital in Spokane and had two stents put in my heart at that time.

— 26 —
Idaho

In January of 2002, I crossed into Idaho on Interstate 90, past the big blue and white sign that welcomes travelers to Idaho, pulled in to the visitor's center, walked into the building, and was greeted by a friendly woman with a rosy face and twinkling eyes, leaning on the counter. Around her were pamphlets, postcards and posters. Her name was Skip.

"May I help you?" she asked, "May I get you some brochures?"

"I thought this was the potato state," I said, with a smile and a nod to a poster claiming "Idaho: the Human Rights State."

———•———

Since my first ride on Blackie, I had been in love with horses: listening to Hop-along Cassidy and the Lone Ranger on the radio, watching Roy Rodgers, Wild Bill Elliot, and the Cisco Kid at the movies and, as I grew older, taking every opportunity to get on a horse's back, and eventually to raise and train my own horses. When I arrived in Coeur d'Alene, Idaho to attend a horse clinic, I owned three horses. I was here to attend "Hoof Talk," a clinic dealing with the health and training of horses.

Initially, when I told Amy where I was going, she was alarmed to say the least. "Do you know who's up there," she protested, followed by a litany of all she had heard about the Aryan Nations in the pages of the Southern Poverty Law Center's news bulletins that she had subscribed to for years.

"Huh?" I said, "So what?" dismissing her fears. "I've been around those kinds of people all my life."

And off I went.

On my first evening in Coeur d'Alene, the front desk clerk at the hotel where I was staying told me that I had a message. I thought it was kind of odd. Who knew I was there other than Amy?

The message told me that there was a ticket for the Human Rights Banquet at the Best Western only a block from the hotel where I was staying. Dressed in my best western clothes, I made my way there and found myself seated at the North Idaho College (NIC) table with Skip who had sent the ticket, along with other lovely people. I met folks from the Coeur d'Alene tribe. I met Debra whose husband was Apache. And adding to the unexpected diversity of people I was meeting, the live music was provided by a family in which the father was Black, the mother white, and the kids—a mix of the two.

This was great! I had not gone to Idaho looking for Nazis. But, on the other hand, who knew that people there would be so friendly. So positive. So diverse.

The first two days of the horse clinic had gone well. Leslie, the main star of the show, thought she had met me previously. "I've seen you before judging a horse show," she mistakenly claimed, and from then on referred to me as, "Judge." Apparently, she had me confused with another Black man who had judged a horse show.

I called Amy enthusiastically at the end of the second day. I told her about going to a pow-wow on the reservation, the human rights banquet, and the horse clinic. I was excited, bubbling over with news and information about Coeur d'Alene—the people and the beauty of the place. It was toward the end of my visit that I had an experience that really shaped the next chapter of my life.

Driving around Lake Coeur d'Alene, sparkling in the sunlight, I took a break and watched two men fish, when an eagle swooped down from the treetops and plucked a fish out of the blue water. The scene reminded me of some things from my past: the river, my father, the

Native American part of my ancestry, and the nickname that my father sometimes called me, "Albert Running Water." It all seemed to come together. At that moment, an idea took shape in my mind, "This is the place that I should be."

From that scene to the practicality of moving to Idaho, many things had to happen: we visited the Coeur d'Alene area four times in different seasons, studied real estate possibilities, talked to folk, and assessed our comfort level as a mixed couple in the area.

On one visit in spring, I remember thinking that the black leather jacket that I had brought as a warm jacket was quite inadequate for the cool wind blowing off Lake Coeur d'Alene. On another visit around New Year we drove on to the Coeur d'Alene reservation in a blizzard wondering if we could cope with the extreme seasonal changes that we would be facing in a move from California to Idaho.

As we drove around the town of Coeur d'Alene, the lack of diversity was almost startling compared to Southern California, The mix of ethnicity that I had first encountered was an anomaly. People of the Coeur d'Alene Indian tribe were seldom seen in the town. But we kept on looking for a black or a brown face, and when we did see someone, we would point them out to each other in pleasure and engage any person of color in conversation when the opportunity arose. Amy made friends with a charming young Black woman who was vigorously pushing shopping carts together in a Safeway parking lot. She met another Black woman in Fred Meyer's and blurted out that she was married to "a brother," only to be told by the woman, "My husband is white."

When it came time to seriously hunt for a house, there were some unexpected quirks. I wanted SPACE. No more California-style living with enormous houses squeezed onto eternally shrinking lots, like the Temecula house we were still living in as we began to explore Idaho. Our home was a beautiful house of over 3,000 square feet, but it was too big and pretentious and did not reflect who we were. It also had a mortgage of well over $2,000 per month and with both of us retiring, this was way beyond our budget. So that translated into looking for a

Home in Athol, all spruced up in white.

more modest home if we wanted the 15 to 20 acres of flat land that was important to me for our horses.

2002 was a good year to be looking for a home in Idaho but sellers or would-be sellers were often just trying out the market and didn't really know if they were ready to sell or not. One house on the Prairie, as it is called, was perfect for our needs. It was a relatively new house in excellent condition on flat land with a barn, corrals, and fields out back that could be rented out, plus it boasted an enormous moose head mounted over the fireplace, claiming its territory. We put in an offer on a Friday and the owner took it off the market at the weekend. He had just been tentatively poking his toe in to the waters of the real estate market.

Another home off Highway 54, looked good on the internet, but the inside the house was a warren of small, brown rooms that needed lots of work. Dressed from head to toe in brown to match the interior of her house, the owner was inordinately proud of her home. In addition to the depressing interior, the rights to water from the well was problematic in that some surrounding land was to be portioned off and sold and the water to the newly established lots would come from the property we were looking at. It sounded complicated and very tenuous.

After looking at six or seven properties our nerves were getting a little frayed. I grew tired of our well-intentioned but very chatty real estate agent whose driving became quite erratic as she talked and gesticulated. I had taken to following our real estate agent's car in my truck while Amy rode with her. I gave rather terse responses to her cheerful questions when we toured a house.

Finally, we came to a possibility. Sitting among tall trees, down a long winding driveway, sat a brown ranch-style house. There was quite a bit of level ground for horses, and it was a 15-acre lot. Inside, the walls were too gloomy for my taste, but the living space was open with, if not exactly a soaring ceiling, at least some height.

And so, we both agreed on the home we purchased for quite different reasons. Amy was looking at the potential in the home—I saw the potential in the land. Neither of us looked at the work involved in clearing brush, cutting down dead trees, cutting trails, and establishing horse corrals. We didn't consider the painting, installing flooring, renovating the kitchen and bathrooms, replacing wiring and plumbing that came with the territory.

Neither of us thought about growing older on property that needed a lot of work to maintain it. We didn't care that the house sat north of "the snow line." We didn't consider any future health complications of age. We were 60 and 67 respectively—just young things.

We were up for the challenge!

— 27 —
Life in Athol

O nce we moved in to our new home near the small township of Athol, we cleared land removing over one hundred trees to open up the property to sunlight. There was so much undergrowth of brush that I had to hire some help because I didn't have all the tools to get the clearing done. I made tracks for walking through the property, because Amy wanted a place to walk Buster, our dog, and I wanted to be able to walk the horses down a trail as well. I got the land leveled as much as I could and planted alfalfa in the back pasture to augment hay for the horses. I also bought a lot of equipment for managing our new ranch. It wasn't nearly as big as the ranch in California where we had leased corrals, but this ranch was ours, and all the work was also ours to do.

It took a year for the horses that had been transported up from California to acclimate to the colder climate. For the first winter, the horses were shivering so much that you would have thought someone plugged in an electric wire to them, and I made so many trips to the feed store that clerks there soon knew me by name.

After the first year, Amy got an adjunct teaching job at North Idaho College, and I lectured in her classroom. Amy also did lectures on the Scottish poet Robert Burns and produced Celtic concerts. As for me, I did numerous Buffalo Soldier lectures all over the area, at Fort Sherman on the NIC campus and at local schools. When I did a presentation at Hayden Public Library (Hayden was the precise part of the area that housed the Aryan Nations' international headquarters),

Albert's involvement with the history of the buffalo soldiers spanned many years and allowed him to meet celebrities such as actor Herb Jeffries (above) at The Autry Museum of the American West in Los Angeles. Jeffries, also known as "The Bronze Buckaroo," played a singing cowboy in early westerns.

I was really scared, so some friends brought their concealed weapons with them to make sure I was safe while I was speaking.

The crowd who attended this presentation looked like they had all died the week before. I said, "When you see a person that looks like me, what is the first thing that comes to your mind?"

I was standing right beside a lady who said, "Watermelon."

I said, "OK. How do you feel after saying that?"

She replied, "OK." Another person raised their hand and said, "Fried chicken."

"Can you see a guy like me on a horse as a buffalo soldier riding to protect white settlers with a chicken leg in one hand and spitting out watermelon seeds as he rides?" I asked, adding, "Go ahead and laugh because that's funny!"

They laughed and then I went on to give my history presentation on buffalo soldiers. I always tried to use humor to wake people up and get them to relax.

———— ◆ ————

One day when I was buying wood, I ran into a man who I had seen once before at Burger King. I had chaps on from riding and my western hat. This guy said, "What kind of person are you? You dress different." I replied that I rode horses.

"Were you in Vietnam? What were you—a night fighter? I bet you didn't need any camouflage." I was taken aback by his last comment and walked away.

Another day I was at the local supermarket, I came out with my groceries and saw a truck load of wood. The driver of the truck saw me eyeing it and said, "Is there something wrong with my truck?"

I said, "No," and asked, "What are you doing with all that wood?" He came back with the invitation to tell him where I lived, and he would deliver it. In fact, he followed me home. When we pulled into the driveway to unload the wood, Amy came out to greet us and joked, saying, "Hi, I'm the ranch hand."

He said, "I'll be damned, a tanner and a white ranch hand." He offered to split the wood for me, but I wanted him to get off my property after hearing him use a racial slur, so I said no.

As he left Amy teased saying, "Look at that, you're a tanner."

And I said, "And you're the ranch hand."

The racial comments seemed to increase with time or perhaps I was just growing tired of hearing them, and this made our Idaho journey bitter sweet. We started seeking out people who were kind to us and with whom there were no immediate red flags. Our network grew to about fifty people who we felt were OK and safe to socialize with.

———— ◆ ————

The Aryan Nations was an active and serious threat during our first few years in Idaho. They had an annual parade on Sherman Avenue.

Aryan Nation's last parade downtown Coeur d'Alene, 2004.

All the businesses on this main street closed to show disapproval of the event, but we went down to protest the parade with Skip and friends Karl and Judy. I was wearing a San Diego shirt. This Nazi, in full Nazi regalia, came up to me and said, "I knew it! Outsiders! This man came all the way up from San Diego!"

Amy, who was being provocative in protest to the Nazis, came up and kissed me on the cheek. I told her to not do that again! A young family, all with blond hair, and including two little kids were standing in front of us and, as the parade passed, all gave the Nazi salute. Another fellow singled me out and said, "I'm sorry that we took you out of Africa. We took you out of your homeland and took care of you for all those years." Adding, "God told me to say this to you."

The Aryan Nations took my picture and put it up front on their rally call, saying "Outside agitators are coming up to oppose us."

Richard Butler, their esteemed leader, who had appeared at this

186

rally sitting in a lawn chair on the back of a pickup truck, died soon after this parade.

In various circumstances, it seemed that I was greeted more readily when Amy was with me. One day I went to a Democratic Club lunch meeting on my own. Usually, they would welcome new people at the beginning of the meeting, but on this day, no one looked at me or talked to me. I was discouraged, but Amy said, "Don't give up yet."

The following week, I returned to the Iron Horse on Sherman Avenue for the Democratic Club luncheon. Before they got around to introducing people, I raised my hand and said, "I have a question. Is this a social club or a political club? I was here last week and wasn't recognized at all."

"Oh! Oh! We are so sorry. We just didn't see you."

I thought, "Yah, right…" But I got more involved since they eventually included me. In time, Amy and I got really involved in the Kootenai County Democrats.

In 2006, around the time Senator Obama was thinking about running for office, the club said that it was going to have a training session for Democrats in February. I was asked by a friend to come on down to the event. So, I went to the training at the Red Lion Inn in Post Falls. Initially, I was there to just see what was going on, but everyone else was there to be trained to work in the Kootenai County Democrats.

They were trying to select people to campaign for different candidates. We had some practice runs where we had to give little speeches, and then it came time in the afternoon to vote for a candidate that we wanted to push.

At first, I was going for this little, white guy who was progressive and had a lot of fire in him. I wasn't sure who Obama was, I didn't go for Hillary, and I didn't like John Edwards. So, we had a straw vote. They had boxes with the candidates' names on it, and you had to drop a straw in it. The only box with no straws (they were clear boxes), was Obama's box. I thought, I hate to see a box with no votes in it, so I dropped my straw in Obama's box.

When we started eliminating people, I started pushing for Barack. Someone said, "You should vote for John Edwards, so he can be the top of the ticket and then Obama could be at the bottom of the ticket."

I said, "I'm not going for that," and started canvassing the other groups to switch from their candidates to Obama. It finally came down to Hillary and Obama, and those were the two candidates we supported in Kootenai County.

When it came to door-to-door canvassing voters, Amy said, "We should knock on doors together."

I said, "I am NOT knocking on doors in Idaho with you."

After her first day of campaigning, she saw my point and said, "Wow, I've never been so scared in my life!" People were slamming doors in her face as soon as they heard the word "Democrat." Imagine if she was there knocking on their door with her Black husband too!

———◆———

In February 2007, we had a Democratic Caucus in the gymnasium at NIC. There was a blizzard that night, and although we had promoted this event very well, the weather was awful, and we knew there was a chance no one would come out. I volunteered as a supervisor, verifying that everyone was doing their work correctly. The caucus started at 5 p.m. and closed at 7 p.m.. I was to make sure that it would close on time. I went outside at 6:30 and there was a line of folk a block long braving a blizzard, snow swirling across the sidewalk where they stood. There was no way I could turn those people away. So, 7 p.m. came and went, and I didn't shut down the voting. I went out again at 7:30 and put a tag on the last person in line and said, "Consider yourself in," and that was the last person we let in to vote.

We had the Obama group and the Hillary group, and when it came voting for delegates, after making my short speech in a bid as delegate, I had 395 votes—the highest number of votes. Amy had also been voted in, so off we went to the state convention in Boise. It was a huge thing.

I was running as a Delegate at Large, not wanting to be confined to one geographic area.

At that time, as delegate, you had to list your ethnicity and everything that identified you—gender, disability, veteran, etc. I qualified for

about every marginalized group that was listed. And then I started to get cold feet. But, I gave my speech anyway, and it was so popular that I won again. All these people said, "Go for it." So, I became a national delegate for the state of Idaho in the most diverse group of delegates they had ever had.

Albert was an Idaho national delegate to the Democratic Convention in 2008 and 2012.

— 28 —

Family, Friends & Foes

Living in Idaho was a life of extremes. We both enjoyed the peace and beauty of our own private space—the ranch tucked away among trees with abundant wildlife: deer, wild turkeys, a few moose, and a herd of elk that appeared on a regular basis, the odd coyote, even evidence of bears, although we never saw one.

Family visited more frequently. Tedd, with his wife Cris and four daughters, Mark stationed in Seattle, Marcia, who lives near Washington D.C., and Lester and his wife Kathy. Amy's family visited from Kent, near Seattle, consisting of Amy's daughter Sheila, John her husband, Max and Olivia. Even Douglas flew up from San Diego with a lady friend. One year, many family members and friends came to celebrate a big July 4th celebration with my mother, Grace, in attendance. She was the star of the show.

Olivia was a frequent visitor, and she loved the ranch. She began coming to spend some time alone with us from the tender age of four, and she and I spent a lot of time doing activities together. I taught her to cook. I would show her how to make cookies and pizza, and fun things like that. She just loved doing any creative activity, indoors or outside; anything I could think of that a young girl might enjoy. She is now in high school and becoming a young lady, but she still remembers our earlier times together and has benefited from some of the things we did.

I always felt really close with Olivia, because from the time she was only months old we bonded in an unusual way. I went to burp her on my shoulder then lifted her above my head. She spit up while I was

laughing—and it came right into my mouth. I was surprised that it tasted OK. After she grew up enough to understand, I told Olivia that the "up-chuck" incident makes us closer than ever!

When Olivia was 5 years old on horseback, I had her stand up on a saddle and hold her arms out to the side. Her mom, Sheila, still has a picture of this. I told her that I stood up on a horse when I was 4 years old, and I did it without a saddle to stand on. She had confidence in me enough to try, and she did it. I had Amy take a photo and we gave Olivia the picture for Christmas, and her mother told her, "Olivia, any time you tell me you can't do anything, I'm going to point to this picture."

Olivia was driving the tractor on my lap when she was 8 or 9 years old—(I had a tractor that had a setting where if you put your foot on the gas it would go and if you lifted your foot it would stop, so it was safe.) I didn't have the chance to do the same things with my other grandchildren, in particular Tedd's daughters, because they lived far away and came so seldom. When they did visit, Amy would always take the grandkids to the beach or paint with them. These were the things I felt grandparents and parents should do with their kids and grandkids to pass on happy memories and useful skills.

Since we moved away from Idaho, we have spent more time with Olivia than our other grandkids, because she lives nearby. Unfortunately,

I have never had any of Tedd's girls with me long enough to do many activities. Tory is now five years old. She calls me every week, and recently, she took the phone to her older sisters and said, "Talk to Grandpa. I tell Tory "Semper Fi," sometimes, and she gives me the Marines' "Oohrah!" She has no inhibitions about it, which makes me happy.

———◆———

In Coeur d'Alene, Amy was at a meeting of the Human Rights Education Institute (HREI) in 2008 and heard a young woman speak. She came home and said, "Albert, you should really come down and hear this lady." She also had viewed some artwork in a local gallery done by the same person, and she told me that there was a collage there called, "AFRIKA" that I should go and see.

The next time I saw the director of HREI at the Democratic Club, he said, "You should meet this lady, Rachel. Wait til you see her; she's really a knockout!" I thought, "Hmm." He said, "She's going to start a Black History program at the Institute, and you should be a part of it."

I hadn't really been impressed with HREI under the last two directors, but I went down to see what all the talk was about. My first stop was the art gallery. Amy was right, Rachel's art was captivating, and I bought the framed print of her collage. It was stunning. And then I met Rachel at HREI and found out she was also a teacher at North Idaho College and was leading a Black History program. I was starting to see why Amy said we would get along.

My friendship with Rachel grew. I noticed she was a very hard worker and a talented artist and organizer. Her programs and leadership at the Institute was top notch, but it seemed at times that there was a lingering sadness about her.

One day, when she was labeling posters for an advocacy exhibit, I asked her about her extended family—did they live nearby, or did she have people there for her? She said it was complicated, and she didn't speak to her family often, which left a hole in her son, Franklin's life, because he didn't have any grandparents to interact with. She knew I fished and had a boat, and she asked if I could take Franklin fishing sometime, like a grandpa would. I said, "If I was Franklin's grandfather, you would be my daughter."

She smiled and said, "That would be nice," and has called me "Dad" ever since. It has been a close relationship that, I believe, has enriched both of us.

We made some good friends in Idaho, some of whom were fascinating. We were close with Frank, who was of the Coeur d'Alene tribe. Frank was struggling to finish his bachelor's degree. He was older, and he didn't think he was smart enough, and, in addition, it intimidated him to be with all the young, white folk at NIC. He also couldn't type, which didn't help! A very kind, compassionate college professor convinced him to finish his bachelor's degree and to go for his master's. She even got some students to help him with typing for a fee.

Frank used to tell me about how the white priests came to his father's family and took the kids away, how his last name was changed because the priest in the schools wouldn't allow them to have an Indian name. They asked his father to pick a name, and his father chose Andrew St. John, but the priest said that he couldn't use the bible as a name source. So the "St" became "Si." His grandfather is buried under St John and his descendants under Si John.

I would listen to Frank's stories with elephant ears because I had heard about all of this in books, but hadn't met a native person who had lived it. He showed me how much land they originally had under the treaty and how the white man had shrunk the land down from 1.4 million acres to 40,000 acres. Of these, two thirds is agricultural land and one third timber, but timber sales are spaced from ten to fifteen years apart. The most interesting detail of the new land allocation was that no Indian owned land that bordered the important Lake Coeur d'Alene.

I saw pictures of Frank and another Native American roping bulls and riding horses. With the coming of the horse into their lives, Indians became horse breeders, riders and "Indian Cowboys" in much the same way Blacks took to riding and horse wrangling and became part of the American West. I felt at home with Frank. He has finished his Master's Degree in Native American Studies. During our time in Idaho, we had his wife Pat and him over to the house several times and became good friends.

———————◆———————

I never knew when something scary was going to happen in Idaho.

One evening, in November, we were getting ready to go to Las Vegas to the Marine Corps Ball. I needed some extra hay for my horses while we were gone, so I found someone advertising round 500-pound bales of hay for $50. He was near Silverwood Theme Park in Athol and close to our ranch.

When I got to his place, it was already dark because winter had already set in. Two other guys were there buying hay. I had my white truck plastered with stickers: Marine Corps, Obama, and pro-Liberal. These three white guys kept staring at me. Once they loaded their hay, they drove off. Then, the owner walked up to me and said, "Boy, you're pretty brave."

"What do you mean?" I said, having a good idea what was going through his head.

"You're driving around with those stickers on your truck." I asked him if that meant he was not going to sell me the hay.

FYI: Some Lousy, Egg Sucking, America Hating, Left Wing, Socialist, BrainDead, Dope Smoking, Welfare Sucking, Child molesting, Waste of Skin, Snuck-up AND Stuck A Barry Sotero (aka OBAMA) Bumper Sticker ON Your CAR! I'm ONLY Letting You KNOW So You CAN Remove it! I'm Sure You were wondering why So many Good Americans were Flipping You OFF! LoL

Note left om Albert's truck while parked in Coeur d'Alene.

"No, I'll get you the hay, but I just wanted to point out that you're pretty brave."

After I paid him, he said, "I don't care what your political affiliation is, we are all in this together, and you can vote for anyone you want to."

Mark, the owner, went on, "I am LDS. That's Mormon. As Mormons, we believe in stock piling food and weapons to take care of our own. And Obama is trying to take away our guns."

By this time I'm frozen. It's about 10 degrees Fahrenheit. I have my gloved hands under my armpits. But the round bale still isn't tied down.

"Do you own a gun?" Mark demanded, in a belligerent voice.

I'm kind of shocked by his tone. Still I answer, "Yes."

"Have you been able to buy ammunition? No, you haven't! The Federal government has bought up all the ammunition. Same thing happened in Germany. History will repeat itself." I don't make any comment, so he continued, "This is a man's world."

I can't let this one go! "Well, what about women?" I asked in a mild tone.

"Between you and me, women should be at home, have babies and keep the house. They don't need to vote."

I came back with, "Well, my wife doesn't feel like that, and I don't feel like that." Then said to myself, "Damn! Let me get out of here because this guy might have a firearm on him." I also thought Amy might be worrying about me. It was a dark, moon-less night and getting late.

Amy was indeed worrying about me and asked me not to go out at night anymore. I said to her. "Yes, I was worried about me too." I felt unsafe with that hay seller and never went back to buy his hay even though it was cheaper and closer to an alternative in Priest Lake.

———— • ————

After we had been in our Idaho home for a short while, I had the idea of extending our front living room/dining room by adding a sunroom over the large deck at the rear of the house. We were anticipating workmen turning up, when Amy called me to the front windows sounding alarmed, "Look there!" There was a small white truck coming down our long driveway with an enormous confederate flag waving from its cab. I went out to confront the driver, a young, skinny dude who claimed that he had no idea of the significance of either the flag or why it would alarm a person who looked like me. His swastika tattoos did not help!

———◆———

There was a profusion of guns in Idaho, as there are in all areas of this country. It just seemed even more "up in your face" there.

Near our house there was a shooting range and we frequently heard rapid gunfire. Nearby a young neighbor practiced riding and shooting from horseback. Friends and acquaintances kept loaded shotguns on hand at their front door, and then there were folks that seemed compelled to show me their weapons. One female friend from the therapeutic warm-water pool where I exercised got me out to her car to show me "something." It turned out to be a pink-handled revolver. She scared me half to death. A white woman, Black man and gun were not a healthy combination in any circumstances!

Another incident involving a gun took place in a Fred Meyer parking lot. I approached a parking space about the same time that a family mini-van swung around to park. I indicated that the driver should take the spot, and then upon parking, the driver, a young, family man, approached me and pointedly opened his jacket to reveal his concealed weapon.

The number of confrontational incidents seemed to multiply exponentially as time went on, and I had a sense of apprehension anytime I was out in public places. I was on guard much of the time.

———◆———

After eleven years, we left Idaho. We were getting older and the place we had was too much upkeep in the winters. The property and especially snow removal was running us both ragged: plowing the long driveway, feeding the horses when the temperature was freezing, shoveling frozen poop out of the stalls. We were no longer enjoying the property as much as we wanted to, and we were working too hard. In addition, the racial climate in the Idaho Pan Handle did not improve with time. Some folks of color began to move in to the area but the attitude towards them had a long way to go.

We decided to look in the Gig Harbor area of Western Washington. We would be a lot closer to Amy's daughter and family and Mark was in Seattle too. We had considered this move earlier, but, at that time, we couldn't sell our place in Idaho for a good price. Now the market was more favorable.

One day, I had a bug in my ear and said, "Amy, let's clean up the place and put the property on the market." And that's what we did. We put it on the market for one day, and it attracted a buyer the same day. The folks that bought the place saw the realtor putting up the sign on Cedar Mountain Road, got the number, called their realtor and told her to get in contact with our realtor. They came to see it the following day.

We worked day and night for 25 days because the buyers wanted to move in quickly—in 28 days. We had tons of stuff to get rid of. We had yard sales and barn sales, with some friends coming over to help us. One weekend we drove over Snoqualmie Pass to look for a place near Gig Harbor. It was crazy. We came over and stayed at the Navy Base on the Kitsap Peninsula and worked from there.

We liked the Gig Harbor area but there was only one house for sale in our price range. We didn't want to do any work on a house; we were so tired from working hard on the house in Idaho. So, we found this place, had the inside repainted, and we moved in. Inside, we ended up not liking a lot of things but luckily we met Ed Serock, a remodeling contractor, through an acquaintance of Amy's at the YMCA.

When I arrived home one day, Ed was in the house. He is a wiry, healthy looking, older white guy, and his vibe and presence were OK, and I said, "One thing. Are you going to lecture us about religion—because

I'm sick of that?" This had happened frequently in Idaho with repair-men, trades people etc.

He said, "I'm a recovering Catholic, so no."

I said, "Good," and he came frequently doing a lot of great work in the house, and it doesn't look anything like it did when we moved in.

It took me a year to recover from the move. I was so tired and run down. It took me a long time get my strength back. I bought a Y membership for Amy and me and started driving quite a long way to Silverdale for my swimming and exercise. It had a lazy river where you could really work your legs. In Silverdale, it was so much more diverse. In Gig Harbor at the Y, I didn't want to sit in the jacuzzi with people who wouldn't even look at me or speak to me. I felt they looked down on me because I was, at that time, one of the very few Black people at the Gig Harbor YMCA.

In 2016, I got really sick. Ed and I had become good friends, and he was very concerned and came over to help me out. I started regaining my strength, going back to the Y at Gig Harbor this time for a program called Live Strong that Amy found for cancer survivors. She had developed breast cancer and had gone through chemo and radiation and then entered this program to help regain her strength.

In 2016, when I started recovering, I said if I recover half as much as my previous strength and can move around, I'm just going to enjoy my life and not put my life on hold. I worked hard to get myself back in physical and mental shape, and I wanted to finish my book and travel and get some other things done. Amy knew of a site where a travel agent sends information when he gets good deals, called 'Travel with Alan', and he sent info on a cruise that was a great price. It was a two month, half-way-around the world voyage.

I told Amy, "Let's go."

She said, "I don't want to be on a boat that long." But I started preparing to go. I needed to live to the fullest. Then, one morning at 5 a.m., she woke me up and said, "I want to go too." So, I got on the phone and secured the last vacancy for her. It was in December, and

I found out my passport had expired. We also had to get a visa for India as well as an updated passport. I ran back and forth to Seattle and finally got all set. We missed the first part of the cruise but finally arrived in Singapore and got on the Holland America Cruise liner. We had been on this same type of ship once on a cruise to Alaska.

Personally, I didn't enjoy Malaysia or India (hot and dirty), but I did enjoy Spain and Portugal. To my surprise, the people were nice. I had been expecting discrimination because of my prejudices against Spain and Portugal due to their practices during colonial expansion. Then when we got to Morocco, I was expecting something like the movie Casablanca, but I was very disappointed.

There were some nasty people on the ship from Holland and South Africa, with a great air of entitlement. I had to stay away from them. We met a few Black people on the cruise—some were OK, and some were kind of phony. We met a couple who were Black Hebrews and the wife and I would talk for hours over breakfast on the ship.

— 29 —

Last Chapter

In 2005, I had been diagnosed in California with a slightly enlarged prostate. They said, "We want to keep an eye on it. Come in next year for an exam." The next year came, but not in San Diego. We were now in Idaho.

I went to the VA in Spokane, and they took my PSA again and checked it. The urologist said that I had an enlarged prostate. "We want to do a biopsy to see if there is cancer there." So, they did that, and it came back positive.

In time, the VA determined that my rapidly advancing prostate cancer was a result of exposure to Agent Orange while I was serving in Vietnam.

At that time, the VA only did radical surgery for removing the prostate gland where they cut you open and stitched you up. I thought I don't want that procedure. I knew of a surgeon in California who did less invasive procedures. This surgeon did robotic surgery at Scripps Hospital in La Jolla, one of the top research hospitals in the country. I contacted her. She said, "I would like to examine you first." I answered that I knew I wanted it done. So, she scheduled me for June in the summer of 2006.

When it was all over, I asked if she had got it all, and she replied that she hoped so. Nothing was certain because there are billions of cells that can't be seen by microscope. It was such a nice hospital; I stayed there three days. When they told me I was going to be discharged, I said, "Do I have to be discharged?" There was a pianist playing in the lobby, there were palm trees and hardwood flooring, you had a menu to order whatever you wanted, and my private room did not look like a hospital room.

———————◆———————

Well, unfortunately the surgeon did not get all the cancer and gradually it has affected my kidneys and is spreading further. I finally got to see an oncologist at the VA in Seattle and they signed me up for a research group and have put me on a new medication.

When I was at the 12-week Livestrong program for cancer survivors, I did improve my strength and endurance but wasn't able to buck hay bales. At least I didn't need my walker to get into the house and didn't end up needing all the handicap accessibility tools which the VA had provided. I told myself I wouldn't let myself get to that state where I must use these things all the time, but I am also not stupid and will use things for assistance if I really need to.

It's taken me awhile to realize that all the treatments and benefits I'm getting were earned by service to my country. I feel sorry for the Vets out there who are not even aware of what's available to them. A former Marine, a good friend of mine, met another veteran who had prostate cancer and didn't know that he could access any services. My friend got him connected with the VA, but it was too late. He died a couple of weeks later. A lot of people just don't know what is available to them and feel discarded after they leave the service. They have trouble rejoining society.

Some service folks are just ignorant about what the country offers them—I was, too, for quite a while. But, looking at all the abuse I've gone through in this country, I said, Hey, I deserve these benefits too. All the PTSD from the military and from being a Black man in America made me realize that this is the only type of reparations I'll be getting.

We associate PTSD with military service and action; but trauma in any form is trauma and can affect a person. Up until maybe the last ten years, I've been affected by childhood PTSD and the trauma of being Black in the U.S.A. It's like being on an unlevel playing field and you're trying to catch up all the time. Someone is constantly trying to push you back and putting obstacles in your way just because of the hate they feel. I think back over my life of nearly eight decades, and it's full of hate. There have been some good things that have happened, and some laws have changed, but there is hate against folks who look like me because of the color of their skin and the texture of their hair.

———— ◆ ————

In November of 2017, my son, Mark, contacted me and said he had been researching on ancestry.com and found Wilkersons that were related through DNA. He found a phone number for an S. Wilkerson and gave it to me. I called, got voicemail, left a message saying who I was and, if he was interested, to give me a call back. When he called back, I found out that Sylvania was the son of my father's brother. We were first cousins, and I was ecstatic! I knew there had to be some family members on my father's side out there in the world, but I hadn't known how to find them.

Green Beret SSG Sylvania Wilkerson, receiving the Bronze Star medal for heroism and the Air Medal for duty in Vietnam while a member of 1st Special Forces Group on Okinawa.

Sylvania Wilkerson, Commander, Chapter 657, Military Order of the Purple Heart, Goldsboro, NC. Being honored at Annual Purple Heart Dinner.

Sylvania had two living sisters, Louise and Minnie and he told me on a phone call about our grandmother and her parents. "Do you know who your great grandfather was?" I replied no. He went on to tell me that he was a white man, a slave owner who impregnated his Black slave and then gave away the child, our grandmother, at birth, because she was "mulatto." The Wilkerson family, which she married into, was made up of free men. The Wilkersons started a church in Walnut Grove in the late 1800's, which is still there today.

When I visited Sylvania in North Carolina, his family was the first military family I had met. Sylvania was one of the first Black Green Berets in the country and earned his first Purple Heart at 18 in the Korean War. All the men and some of the women in his family are in the military or have been, ranked from sergeant to lieutenant colonel. Some of his adult children have studied at Duke and North Carolina State. They are also teachers and just well-educated people, and it made me happy to find this out. Sylvania said, "We are Wilkersons, and this is what Wilkersons do."

This is true. Wilkersons survive and thrive.

I am proud of all of my children and what they have accomplished: Marcia, a Director of Member Growth and Collections at a financial institution in Washington, D.C., Mark is the Area Port Director of Seattle under Homeland Security, and Tedd is a gunnery sergeant in the U.S. Marines. As for me, although I would have like to have succeeded more in my careers and life in general, I came a long way from the boy who began life in Alabama in Jim Crow South, who started school late, stuttered, was dyslexic, and experienced abuse.

Retirement felt very odd to me. All of my life until retirement, I had been in survival mode, trying to live and trying to catch up. This state of feeling one-step-behind shaped my choices and opportunities since I was a little boy, through my teenage years, and my time in the military. After years of survival-mode existence, I stopped trying to catch up and just started to strive for a normal life.

I never thought I would be retired or even reach the age of 80 (the

Top left: Tedd, currently a gunnery sergeant in the Marines, has served in Afghanistan and Iraq.

Top right: Mark was Customs Border Patrol Area Port Director of Seattle, 2010 to 2019.

Middle: Marcia visiting in Idaho. She is a Director of Member Growth and Collections at a financial institution in Washington, D.C.

Bottom: Albert and Mark at Tedd's boot camp graduation.

age I'm writing this now). Through my previous marriages with Maria and Robyn, trying to catch up and do the right thing, I felt very tired mentally. I had to give even when I didn't have anything to give. Still I wanted to create something so I could give back to others and be accepted. All the little things that I had to go through as a child and as a young Marine shaped me. The situations I faced as an older Marine and the challenges I faced becoming a dad before I was ready to be one, also left their mark. There was no manual or playbook for my life, no list of instructions to guarantee the best outcome. I had never taken time to get to know myself and enjoy living.

In retirement, I did a great deal of reflecting upon my new-found freedom. I realized that I had been mentally tired because I had to try to be ahead of everyone else. My dad would always tell me that just to get my foot in the door I had to be ten times better than the white male. I thought, "Why should I have to do that?" But through my life, I saw it. I developed a sense of fighting. I'm going to live and you're not going to take me down.

I realize now that I have had many fears which were instilled early in life. I developed trust issues with people in general, particularly with women. "Women are mean and conniving" was one common, damaging message. I was also afraid of white men who reassembled my white grandfather in any way. With food, I have always bought too much food because of an underlying fear that food is going to run out in the house. And finally money. Through the years I have, at times, been very protective of my money, distrusting others with my finances. Some of these issues were part of being affected by PTSD. I fought hard to overcome this condition and, with the passage of time, and the help of therapy, I have lost much of the hypervigilance and distrust that were part of my life for so long.

Mark, Marcia and Tedd with Albert together for the last time, May 2018.

———◆———

Throughout my life, I was always interested in improving myself and improving the lives of others, particularly children. It took me a long time to really understand how to love myself and embrace life rather than just getting pulled through the years by responsibilities and circumstances. I realized that life is all about choices, and that I could choose to be a victim, or I could choose to learn from my life experiences.

I choose to learn from life!

Keep On Living!

KOL

– 30 –

Epilogue

Albert died on August 15, 2018, as a result of metastatic prostate cancer. His death certificate includes the words, "served on ground in Vietnam. Agent orange exposure."

During the last six months of Albert's life it was clear to both of us that cancer was advancing through his body, however, that did not hold Albert back from living life to the fullest. He had always expressed a desire to return to Vietnam. Once again Travel with Alan came through and advertised a

good price for a trip to Vietnam and Thailand in January of 2018. The ship was small and not quite up to the standard of Holland America Line vessels. Despite this, we had some wonderful experiences, particularly on a Thai island where we visited an elephant compound and rode on the back of an elephant through vegetation along winding sandy trails, and across streams of water. Albert had a great time. He still had the

strength and joie de vivre that had been part of him for his entire life and slid from the seat on the back of our elephant down to the neck of the great beast and rode on his perch, many feet from the ground, then shimmied back up at the end of our ride.

In February, Albert still had the strength and commitment to his ideals of teaching about Black History, when he presented to the Area Port of Seattle (U.S. Customs and Border Protection) in honor of National Black History Month. The presentation included his personal experiences in the military as well as heroic Blacks who fought for our country. Albert's talk was to his usual high standard and was very well received.

———————◆———————

After our return, Albert finally was granted an appointment to a VA oncologist and we got the disturbing news that the metastasized cancer was indeed advancing through his body. Unfortunately the drug he was prescribed was not tolerated well by anyone with a compromised heart, and he had a heart attack in March, followed by another in hospital.

In all, Albert was hospitalized three times in the months March through July. He came home in August to hospice care where he was visited by friends and family. Many folks came to see him, knowing it was for the last time. Both family and friends gave hours and days of care to make his final days full of love and comfort.

I am so glad that I was able to be part of that care giving for Albert as he transitioned from this life. He expressed such tenderness and love that it wiped out all of the pain and distress that is part of watching a loved one die. He even kept his sense of humor to the end!

Some of the traits that kept me fascinated by this man who I knew for thirty years were his sense of humor, charisma, strong moral compass, resilience, and a love of children (babies in particular). Being human, I also miss his incredible cooking!

His spirit is very much still with me and with those who loved him. He lives on in the wonderful memories we made together.

—Amy

AMY C. WILKERSON

Born and raised in Scotland, Amy grew up with a love for her native land. Settling in the U.S., she earned her BA in English and MA in Counseling Psychology and taught for many years in San Diego City Schools.

While living in the Inland Northwest, she taught for several years at North Idaho College, where she also lectured on Robert Burns, national poet of Scotland and produced a series of Celtic concerts in the Coeur d'Alene area, in which she took part, with poetry and storytelling.

Amy was married to Albert for 27 years living in California, Idaho and Western Washington where she now lives. She has an ongoing interest in creative endeavors including writing and painting.